Praise for *The Purpose Revolution*

"A valuable addition to a growing body of academic research showing that purpose-led companies really do perform better, last longer, and are in tune with the hopes and aspirations of the people they serve. This book shows why purpose needs to start at the top and then shows how to embed it everywhere in the organization."
—**Paul Polman, CEO, Unilever**

"Dr. John Izzo is one of the world's leading business authors, and his latest work, *The Purpose Revolution*, shares invaluable lessons on how to build your organization's culture around a common purpose."
—**Darren Entwistle, President and CEO, TELUS**

"This book makes a compelling case for how people are seeking self-actualization through both the work they choose to do as employees and the companies they choose to buy from. It is filled with many useful tools to help define, refresh, and bring purpose to life in your business."
—**Joey Bergstein, CEO, Seventh Generation**

"*The Purpose Revolution* is at once an eloquent manifesto and a practical guidebook. The authors first grab you with compelling evidence that purpose matters (a lot). Then they tell engaging stories about people and organizations who've thrived because they understood at their core how important purpose is. And every step of the way John and Jeff provide immediate actions you and your organization can take to audit, craft, communicate, and commit to an authentic, inspiring, and scalable purpose that connects. *The Purpose Revolution* is here."
—**Jim Kouzes, coauthor of *The Leadership Challenge* and Dean's Executive Fellow of Leadership, Leavey School of Business, Santa Clara University**

"Purpose-driven business is a powerful approach for overcoming our greatest societal challenges and driving business growth. This book provides a realistic, practical approach to embedding purpose in an organization, and it's engaging along the way."
—**Jean Bennington Sweeney, Chief Sustainability Officer, 3M**

"*The Purpose Revolution* provides a powerful blueprint to higher levels of employee engagement and competitive advantage! An amazingly insightful book."
—**Marshall Goldsmith, *New York Times* #1 bestselling author of *Triggers* and *What Got You Here Won't Get You There***

"In *The Purpose Revolution*, Dr. Izzo offers a framework for success that is grounded in research and decades of wisdom accumulated from advising leaders."
—**Dr. Geoff Smart, founder and Chairman, ghSMART, and author of *Who* and *Power Score***

"This powerful, practical book not only shows you what your employees and customers expect but shows you how to powerfully activate purpose in your business. A must-read for anyone wanting to win in the age of social good."
—**KoAnn Vikoren Skrzyniarz, founder and CEO, Sustainable Life Media, producers of Sustainable Brands**

"Purpose and meaning are at the heart of leading. If you have time to read only one book this year on what brings the power of purpose to leadership, this is it!"
—**Richard Leider, international bestselling author of *The Power of Purpose*, *Repacking Your Bags*, and *Life Reimagined***

"At a time when Air Canada is expanding globally, our business is growing at an unprecedented rate, and we have the additional challenge of a multigenerational workforce, John's insightful findings around the value of purpose resonated with us at every level and will inform our culture change initiatives now and in the future."
—**Arielle Meloul-Wechsler, Senior Vice President, People and Culture, Air Canada**

"John Izzo was an early advocate for the idea that companies have a 'soul'—a meaning and purpose beyond just profit-making. In *The Purpose Revolution*, Izzo and Vanderwielen provide a strong business and moral case for business leaders to focus intently on why their companies exist and what they do for society. This book shows you how identifying and acting on your company's purpose will make your business more successful, your employees more engaged, and your own work more meaningful."
—**Andrew Winston, author of *The Big Pivot* and coauthor of *Green to Gold***

THE
PURPOSE
REVOLUTION

Other Books by John Izzo

Awakening Corporate Soul (with Eric Klein)

The Five Secrets You Must Discover Before You Die

The Five Thieves of Happiness

Second Innocence

Stepping Up

Values Shift (with Pam Withers)

THE
PURPOSE
REVOLUTION

HOW LEADERS
CREATE ENGAGEMENT AND
COMPETITIVE ADVANTAGE
IN AN AGE OF SOCIAL GOOD

JOHN IZZO AND
JEFF VANDERWIELEN

Berrett–Koehler Publishers, Inc.
a BK Business book

Berrett-Koehler Publishers, Inc.
1333 Broadway, Suite 1000, Oakland, CA 94612-1921
Tel: (510) 817-2277   Fax: (510) 817-2278   www.bkconnection.com

Ordering Information

Quantity sales. Special discounts are available on quantity purchases by corporations, associations, and others. For details, contact the "Special Sales Department" at the Berrett-Koehler address above.

Individual sales. Berrett-Koehler publications are available through most bookstores. They can also be ordered directly from Berrett-Koehler: Tel: (800) 929-2929; Fax: (802) 864-7626; www.bkconnection.com.

Orders for college textbook/course adoption use. Please contact Berrett-Koehler: Tel: (800) 929-2929; Fax: (802) 864-7626.

Distributed to the U.S. trade and internationally by Penguin Random House Publisher Services.

Berrett-Koehler and the BK logo are registered trademarks of Berrett-Koehler Publishers, Inc.

Printed in the United States of America

Berrett-Koehler books are printed on long-lasting acid-free paper. When it is available, we choose paper that has been manufactured by environmentally responsible processes. These may include using trees grown in sustainable forests, incorporating recycled paper, minimizing chlorine in bleaching, or recycling the energy produced at the paper mill.

Cataloging-in-Publication Data is available at the Library of Congress.

ISBN: 978-1-62656-966-9

25   24   22   21   20   19   18   10   9   8   7   6   5   4   3   2   1

Cover design by Nancy Austin Design. Interior design and composition by Gary Palmatier, Ideas to Images. Elizabeth von Radics, copyeditor; Mike Mollett, proofreader; Rachel Rice, indexer.

Dedicated to my mother, Irene Parisi-Izzo,
who taught me that making a living
was not as important as leaving a mark,
and to the Reverend Dr. Robert Kelley,
who first embodied purpose for me.

JOHN IZZO, PHD

In memory of my father—
who encouraged me to always explore,
to turn from the well-traveled and familiar road
onto the trails, side roads, and backways.
Dad, I continue down the path you charted.

JEFF VANDERWIELEN, PHD

Contents

Preface

THIS IS A BOOK FOR ANY LEADER, CEO, BUSINESS OWNER, ENTRE-
preneur, human resources (HR) executive, consultant, or marketing
professional who wants higher levels of engagement and loyalty from
both employees and customers. If you work for a for-profit company,
this book will show you how to get the lion's share of loyalty from
employees and customers; if you are in the nonprofit or government
sector, it will show you how to harness purpose to fulfill your mission.

This book describes a revolution of expectations of what we want
from those we work for, buy from, and invest in, and it provides a
practical blueprint for creating a significant competitive advantage by
embedding purpose in your leadership and organization. While CEOs
and business owners can use this book to help determine the direction of the organization and how to shape corporate culture, leaders
at all levels, including frontline managers, will find it a practical guide
to engaging employees and customers around purpose while finding
more meaning in their own work.

In 1994 John Izzo coauthored a book titled *Awakening Corporate
Soul: Four Paths to Unleash the Power of People at Work* in which he
suggested that those companies that have a deep purpose and are
socially responsible will ultimately be more successful than those
that follow a typical path focused on profits. The idea was mostly
aspirational—a vision of how business might be—because at the time
only a small number of companies viewed social responsibility or
purpose as a primary path to success.

Although it feels like moral high ground to be ahead of the
curve, over the ensuing 20 years it still seemed like this trend was
growing, albeit quite slowly. Many companies were intrigued about

adding "doing good" and "purpose" to their to-do list, but it was rarely a major priority in most enterprises. Today that's changing—and it's happening fast.

In recent years a quiet revolution has been brewing around the globe. Cutting across geography, generation, and sector, there is a sea change in terms of what employees, customers, and investors expect from business. Employees want a meaningful job, where they not only get a paycheck but make a difference; customers want to consume with less guilt about the impact of their purchases on society and the planet, leveraging good if they can; and investors are beginning to see that doing good is simply good business.

These three groups still want what they have always wanted, of course: Employees want a great salary and a career path; customers want quality, innovation, and value; and investors want to make a return. But the revolution we write about is in many ways a revolution about *and* instead of *or*. We want all of these things *and* we want our work, our buying, and our investing to help leverage a better world. We call this desire for meaning and doing good *purpose*.

When we first began writing this book, a colleague who is steeped in the emerging revolution of expectations said to us, "This sounds like a book that was written five years ago!" His point was that most business leaders know about the growing focus on purpose, so there was a danger that this book felt like old news. On the one hand, this is true. As we travel around the world, working with major companies and attending gatherings of business leaders, the words *purpose, sustainability, social good,* and the like are now common sentiments expressed in many business circles. Most every major business has a portal on its website to tell you how much good it is doing in the world and touting its purpose to make a difference for customers and employees. So why does this book matter?

There are two reasons why we feel this book is sorely needed. The first is because, for most companies, purpose and social good are still seen as just one of many trends driving the success or failure of their business. We believe that most leaders have no idea how pervasive and important the emerging focus on purpose is and how it will reshape everything about how we do business. In this book we show how this revolution is not just another wave about to hit the shores of your organization but is literally the most important wave of our generation. We hope to make the compelling case that this may be *the* biggest business opportunity of our time.

Second, this book is needed because even though most leaders now say that purpose and social good matter to their business, they are failing to truly embed purpose in their leadership, and few companies are truly reorienting their business. The purpose of this book is to show you both the shape of the coming revolution and, more importantly, how your business—and you as a leader—must change to thrive in the age of social good.

Over the past 20-plus years, we have worked with about 550 companies around the globe, helping them become more purpose driven. We have learned a great deal about why some companies and leaders are thriving in this new era and what we must do to truly harness the power of these new desires for good. Much of what we share comes from our own consulting work.

For this book we also embarked on a journey to find out how companies were winning in the revolution and what it might say about how to succeed and do good. We surveyed hundreds of leaders to ask what keeps them up at night. We interviewed leaders at more than 50 companies who are making real progress on purpose, including leaders from 3M Company, Ford, Hewlett-Packard (HP), IBM, Seventh Generation, and TELUS.

Another very important source for the research in this book comes from a larger research project that Andrew Winston (author of *The Big Pivot: Radically Practical Strategies for a Hotter, Scarcer, and More Open World* and co-author of *Green to Gold: How Smart Companies Use Environmental Strategy to Innovate, Create Value, and Build Competitive Advantage*) and John Izzo are conducting to interview CEOs who have demonstrated real leadership and success in driving social good. Andrew and John have interviewed 18 of them, including Inge Thulin of 3M, Ahmet Muhtar Kent of Coca-Cola, William Clay Ford Jr. of Ford Motor Company, Darren Entwistle of TELUS, Joey Bergstein of Seventh Generation, Donald Arthur Guloien of Manulife Financial, and Paul Polman of Unilever. Although that research is focused mostly on how these CEOs became committed to sustainable leadership, we share some of it here as it relates to how they see the purpose revolution and what leaders must do to succeed in this new reality.

We sought advice from some of the thought leaders who are shaping this movement, many of whom we quote in this book. In each case we asked three basic questions:

 ■ What is changing in terms of expectations around purpose and social good?

 ■ What is your company doing to respond to those shifts, and what is working?

 ■ What should other leaders and organizations be doing to truly embed purpose?

Wherever we don't cite a specific reference, the quotes and information come directly from these interviews. We felt it would be redundant to make that clear in each instance.

Part one, "Harnessing the Power of Purpose," focuses on the *why*. We show why this is truly a revolution, help you understand the three waves of the purpose trend and what's driving it, and then share the keys to fostering an organization or team focused on purpose and social good. You also learn why most leaders are currently failing to embed purpose in their teams. Part two, "Leading a Purpose-Driven Culture," focuses on the *how*. We provide a practical blueprint for how to lead for purpose, as well as give you scores of useable ideas—from those already thriving—on how you can engage purpose in your team and company. We think every leader has a critical role to play in driving a purpose culture. The book is meant to be eye opening but also practical.

Throughout the book we provide numerous exercises to help you gain insight into personal and company purpose. These activities consist of actionable advice that you can implement at work and steps to help you close the purpose gap, activate purpose, and create a purpose-driven culture. We ask you to take notes, brainstorm ideas, and write down your thoughts, so we suggest obtaining a dedicated notebook for the exercises. Of course, you are free to use a digital mobile device—just make sure it's something you can access easily for your reference.

It might be useful to give some advice on how to read and use this book. Dividing it into two parts was a deliberate choice. Part one is of most interest to CEOs, business owners, HR leaders, marketing leaders, chief sustainability officers, and consultants because it shows why purpose matters and helps you understand the emerging shifts in expectations around purpose. If you are a midlevel or frontline operational leader, you will want to understand these trends but may find part two, which focuses on how to embed purpose into your leadership, even more helpful. If you are the CEO, owner, or a senior division leader, you may find it useful to encourage every leader to read the book and focus on part two. Business books aren't always meant to be read cover to cover, and readers should focus on the sections most compelling and relevant to them.

When John wrote *Awakening Corporate Soul,* it was about not just doing good business but also how business could do good. Make no mistake, this new book is *not* just about winning employees and customers; it is about the soul of business. Ever since we began advising companies, we have believed that business could help foster a more equitable and sustainable world for communities and the planet.

The Purpose Revolution is ushering in a great opportunity for you as a leader to create meaningful competitive advantage not only in terms of winning employee commitment, keeping top talent, and gaining extraordinary loyalty from customers, as well as investment from investors, but also by stepping up to focus on social good. You have a chance to be part of a revolution that will shape the world our children and grandchildren will live in.

Are You Ready for the Purpose Revolution?

T HERE IS A REVOLUTION HAPPENING IN BUSINESS RIGHT NOW, and for you as a leader it is one of the greatest opportunities of our generation. It is a movement that is already well under way. It's global, and those leaders who take it seriously will be able to engage employees and customers, leading to sustainable success for years to come. Those who ignore it will become irrelevant. This book is a guide to thriving in what we call the *purpose revolution*.

The revolution is a shift among employees, customers, and investors who expect businesses to meet their self-oriented needs while being a force for good in society and the environment. In the case of employees, it also constitutes a growing expectation that work becomes a place of fulfillment, where one can make a difference in the world while also finding personal meaning and satisfaction.

This revolution is in part a reaction to a shift that occurred in the 1970s, as companies began putting greater emphasis on shareholder return as the prime directive, with customers, employees, communities, and other stakeholders falling by the wayside. This trend flourished throughout the '80s, '90s, and early 2000s on the assumption that because stockholders "own" the companies in which they invest, they should have the final say and that it's a company's duty to do all that it can to support shareholder value. Today wise companies are realizing that their actions affect many more people, directly and indirectly, than just their short- or long-term investors. More importantly, these companies are seeing that employees, customers, and investors are expecting something different.

WHAT IS PURPOSE ANYWAY?

The word *purpose* has started showing up with great frequency in corporate circles around the world. For example, in a 2016 report on the global state of purpose, Ernst & Young noted that "public discourse about 'corporate/organizational purpose' has increased fivefold since 1994, now trending at an exponential rate that surpasses the rate of public discourse about sustainability."[1] *Purpose* can be defined for both the individual and the organization. For the individual employee or worker, purpose is the belief that work serves to make a difference in a way that is meaningful to that person. It is the part of work that is not simply about earning a salary or having status but a sense that the work itself has meaning, with an underlying feeling that the job serves society or their personal values in a positive way.

The Japanese have a word for this sense of purpose, *ikigai,* which is one's "reason for being," similar to the French phrase *raison d'être.* Everyone, according to the Japanese, has *ikigai.* Finding it requires a deep and often lengthy search of self. Such a search is regarded as very important because it is believed that discovery of one's *ikigai* brings satisfaction and meaning to life. Examples include work, hobbies, and raising children. One of our executive-coaching clients in Japan tells us that there is a growing reimagining of the meaning of work occurring in that culture. We believe that this emerging desire to find *ikigai* at work is global.

For organizations we define *purpose* as an aspirational reason for being that is about making life better now and in the future for all stakeholders, especially customers, society, and the planet. A *purposeful organization* is one that has built its entire enterprise around this core reason for existence. Though the organization may manufacture products, provide services, and generate profits, its entire system revolves around this desire to make life better for customers, employees, society, and the environment now and in the future.

Though profits are a prime focus for most companies, almost all profits are the result of fulfilling a purpose that serves customers. Yet many businesses today are disconnected from that sense of purpose, leaving profits as the end goal rather than as a measure of fulfilling the needs of those they serve.

The Purpose Gap

There is little doubt that the emerging employee, customer, and investor is increasingly driven by a desire for purpose, and we demonstrate that with facts in the pages that follow. But in this new world of social good, there is a gap between these emerging expectations and what business is delivering. We call this the *purpose gap.* In business *gap* means opportunity: if people want something and organizations are not delivering it, those organizations that close the gap between expectations and delivery will succeed.

Most companies are currently failing at providing purpose to their employees, customers, and investors, or they are at least suboptimizing its potential. Research shows that almost 70 percent of employees say the company they work for is mostly interested in profits and serving its own needs rather than those of its customers or society. Compare this statistic to the 86 percent of employees who "believe it's important that their own employer is responsible to society and the environment, with over half (55 percent) feeling it is very important,"[2] and the 60 percent who want their work to have purpose, and it's obvious to see that a meaningful gap exists.

Furthermore in a large study of CEOs, the majority said they thought that activating purpose would drive higher employee satisfaction (89 percent), the company's ability to transform (84 percent), and the ability to increase customer loyalty (80 percent). Yet only about 45 percent said they were doing well at embedding purpose in their companies.[3] They struggle to communicate how the jobs they provide offer purpose and meaning beyond monetary or transactional value.

Job seekers looking for purpose are not given clear connections to how their work contributes to something more substantial or how it has a positive impact on others. Business leaders are expected to play a central role in connecting work to purpose, but it has been shown that less than one-third help their direct reports connect their own purpose to the work of the company.[4]

This gap represents a major opportunity. The fact that talent wants purpose—but most employees perceive companies as primarily being interested in their own welfare rather than that of the customer or society—means that those organizations that find a way to truly connect to purpose will gain a meaningful advantage. Whether you're a CEO, a midlevel manager, an HR recruiter, or a small-business owner, understanding and building a purpose-focused team will lead to higher long-term performance throughout your organization.

Purpose and the War for Talent

As we interviewed leaders while writing this book, they repeatedly told us that when they visit college campuses the reputation of their organization for doing good is a major driver for top talent. Andrew Harding, chief executive of the Chartered Institute of Management Accountants, commented on the changing expectations of the new workforce: "Now conversations with undergraduates are 'I want to work in a real business, I want to see the value of that business and I want to be able to feel I am part of delivering that value.' This is a very, very fundamental mind-set shift that plays alongside your organizational purpose and agenda."[5]

The purpose-centered employee is transforming the rules about why we work and the role of business in our lives and society. Thirty-seven percent of the global workforce is now purpose oriented, and the number is growing.[6] This transformation—happening from the inside out—is based on personal values and is driving three big shifts in the workplace.

One shift is from working for money to *having a job with purpose,* a reorientation to one's relationship to the job, moving away from work as merely a means to make a living toward its being an expression of personal values. Purpose and meaning are the main themes. The second shift is an expectation that the workplace will enrich the lives of its employees, providing opportunities for people to contribute beyond the job itself—*an opportunity to make a difference at work,* either inside or outside the company. Enrichment, growth, and contribution are paramount. The third shift is a redefinition of the role of business in society: *the company needs to make the world a better place.* Together these transformations are shaping new relationships among employees, companies, and society.

Offering purpose in a job is no longer a nice-to-have benefit to lure top talent but now the required ante to play in the high-stakes game of talent acquisition. Drew Bonfiglio, cofounder and managing partner of Emzingo, a development leadership company that works with young talent, has firsthand experience with the new purpose-driven employee. He told us, "You have to make purpose intrinsic to the company culture."

Jean Bennington Sweeney, chief sustainability officer at 3M, echoed the same sentiment about its workforce: "Our employees want a job with purpose; they need to see a purpose bigger than themselves when they come into work."

The job of leaders in the age of social good is to *activate purpose,* meaning they help bring out the latent good intentions and aspirations of employees to make a difference in the lives of others, society, and the environment and then translate those objectives into viable strategies and actions across the organization. But they don't stop there. In addition to embedding purpose throughout the organization, they must also find consistent ways to focus customers and investors on the company's authentic story of doing good.

Your Customers Want Purpose

Though employees have been the fastest to embrace the purpose revolution, customers are quickly coming around. The situation for customers is more complicated than for employees because who you work for is a binary choice, whereas consumers may use hundreds of products and services during a given year. Customers' reasons for buying products from specific companies are complex, including product effectiveness, style, social status, cost, value, and speed. Whether the product is also good for the world or provides a sense of purpose is one of numerous factors considered.

That said, 60 percent of customers today report making socially conscious buying decisions; 83 percent of customers rate that buying from a green company is important to them.[7] A 2015 report showed that "66 percent of global consumers say they're willing to pay more for sustainable brands."[8] Heath Shackleford, founder and kick-starter of Good.Must.Grow., noted that "consumers are aligning their purchasing habits with their passion and purpose and more aggressively supporting socially responsible businesses."

The emerging global customer wants what we call *and*. They want the product to meet their self-oriented needs at a fair value *and* they want to purchase "without guilt," leveraging a better world through their buying habits. Yet there are barriers to acting on those desires. According to a 2015 global survey of human aspirations by GlobeScan and BBMG, more than half of global customers say it matters to them whether the companies they buy from are socially responsible and green, yet customers say they are routinely confused about whether the brands they buy are "good."[9]

In other words, there is a similar purpose gap for customers who increasingly want to "buy with purpose" but feel they don't have the information they need to choose wisely. Given that confusion it should come as little surprise that consumers also say they wouldn't care if 70 to 75 percent of the brands in the world disappeared—a sign that customers believe that most brands are not acting responsibly or sustainably.[10] Consumers want to buy from companies they believe in. Those companies that can tell an authentic story of purpose are winning customers, but few companies are doing this.

The purpose-centered customer is highly connected, living in a world of mobile and social media where information moves at the speed of light, creating a "new world of peer-to-peer commerce where *People Rule.*"[11] Customers around the globe have instant access to information about a company and the power to express, in that moment, their brand experience to a receptive worldwide audience.

The 2015 global survey identified an emerging group that it has named "Aspirationals" as the largest and most significant consumer group in the world.[12] This group differs from "Advocates," who are focused most on buying fewer things and living as green a lifestyle as possible. According to the report, Aspirationals matter because they are the first to unite materialism, sustainability values, and cultural influence, making them an essential audience to build markets, influence cultural norms, and shape behavior change at scale. This group likes to buy, but they want to buy with purpose. Most Aspirationals—70 percent—said that companies should be accountable for "ensuring their products and operations do not harm the environment."

An international study by UK-based Unilever reveals that one-third of consumers (33 percent) are now choosing to buy from brands they believe are doing social or environmental good.[13] The study suggests that an estimated €966 billion opportunity exists for brands that make their sustainability credentials clear.

The study asked 20,000 adults from five countries how their sustainability concerns affect their choices in stores and at home. Crucially, it then mapped their claims against real purchasing decisions, giving a more accurate picture than ever before of what people are actually buying—and why. More than one in five (21 percent) of the people surveyed said they would actively choose brands if they made their sustainability credentials clearer on their packaging and in their marketing.

The scale of this opportunity is further borne out by Unilever's own financial performance. Of its hundreds of brands, those such as Dove, Hellmann's, and Ben & Jerry's that have integrated sustainability into both their purpose and their products delivered nearly half the company's global growth in 2015. Collectively, they are also growing 30 percent faster than the rest of the business.

The study also suggests that the trend for purpose-led purchasing is greater among consumers in emerging economies than in developed markets. While 53 percent of shoppers in the United Kingdom and 78 percent in the United States say that they feel better when they buy products that are sustainably produced, that number rises to 88 percent in India and 85 percent in both Brazil and Turkey.

So, while it is fair to say that employees *are in,* we might say customers *want in;* that is, the trend toward customers' wanting to leverage good with their purchases is growing—and fast—all around the globe. Those businesses that can make it easy for people to "choose good" will have a true advantage. The final group you need to consider, however, is the investor.

Investors: Do They Really Care about Purpose?

While employees are showing that they care about purpose with the choices they make and customers are showing that they want to buy with purpose, it is important to ask if investors are really interested in doing good. Early signs suggest that investors are starting to get serious about purpose, such as impact investing, where people make choices to invest in businesses that have social impact as a major focus of their reason for existence. For example, in 2007 approximately 11 percent of US-managed assets ($2.71 trillion) were invested in socially responsible investing (SRI) products—an 18 percent increase from the previous decade.[14] The US SIF Foundation reported that in just three years, from 2012 to 2015, assets in sustainable and responsible mutual funds grew from $60.1 billion to $85.4 billion.[15]

In a 2015 survey of investors and executives across 113 countries, MIT Sloan in partnership with the Boston Consulting Group reported that 73 percent of investors said that sustainability performance mattered more than it did three years earlier.[16] Major pension funds have also increasingly started using their weight to push companies to address problems such as climate change. Risk mitigation issues around environment and society are also becoming a major focus of large investors. Yet research shows that while most investors want to leverage good with their investment choices, making a solid return on those investments is still the critical driver.

The investor role in the purpose revolution has two elements adding to its force, potentially making it ultimately even more powerful than consumers or employees. One element is the data: business performance numbers increasingly show that companies that are run sustainably *outperform* nonsustainable companies. Second, investors are realizing that there is more inherent risk in nonsustainable companies compared with those with sustainable practices. In short, sustainably run companies are a better investment than nonsustainable companies. Together the combined energy underlying the investor role— social and moral values, better performance, and lower risk—is powering a push toward purpose.

Socially and environmentally minded investors are now having an impact on business practices as well. It has been reported that the number of shareholder proposals filed on environmental and social issues has increased by 50 percent in the past 10 years.[17] In another study George Serafeim and Calvert Research and Management found that more than 80 percent of the withdrawal agreements negotiated with companies on environmental issues from 2008 to 2010 had been fully or substantially implemented.[18]

A number of SRI firms and public pension funds filed shareholder proposals regarding the environmental impact of fracking with Chevron, ExxonMobil, EQT Corporation, EOG Resources, Pioneer Natural Resources, and Occidental Petroleum Corporation. And they got results. For example, ExxonMobil agreed to initiate reporting on risk management across 26 categories; EQT agreed to measure and disclose methane leakage and report progress on reducing risks to ground and surface water; Pioneer Natural Resources agreed to environmental, social, and governance (ESG) oversight of its board charter and increased disclosures on water sourcing, recycling, and air emissions management; and Occidental Petroleum agreed to report on its recycling, water consumption, waste management, and toxic chemical reduction progress.[19]

Employees are already in, customers want in, and investors are thinking about coming in. The investor component of the revolution may clearly be lagging the other two, but there is a good chance that once it gains momentum investors will join employees and customers to become an awesome force that will hit businesses at all levels. As one mutual fund manager told an audience at a large Sustainable Brands conference in San Diego in 2016, "When investors get religion on this issue—and they will—companies are going to be scrambling to catch up."

REVOLUTIONS CREATE WINNERS AND LOSERS

Human history has always been shaped by revolutions. Whether the agricultural revolution, the Enlightenment, the industrial revolution, violent revolutions that swept in democracy in places like France and the United States, or the revolutions in China and Russia that birthed socialism and communism, human progress is often punctuated by major shifts. Our business and social lives are equally shaped by revolutions, in both popular thought and technology. Looking back only 50 years, it's hard to believe how drastically the most integral aspects of our lives have changed, whether considering food, entertainment, communications, social interaction, or commerce.

When revolutions occur, there are almost always winners and losers. Consider one of the greatest business revolutions of the past 50 years: the quality revolution. In the 1960s management thinkers W. Edwards Deming and Joseph Juran espoused ideas about how to manage quality by looking at processes rather than people and by creating a corporate culture that put improvement at the center of the enterprise. Their ideas got little traction in the United State and Europe but found a more receptive audience in Japan.

By the time 1970 rolled around, the quality revolution had taken hold, and Japanese products were both relatively inexpensive and the highest-quality manufactured goods in the world. Products once considered "cheap" were now at the top of *Consumer Reports* assessments of reliability and quality. By 1975 everyone knew that the best cars in the world were manufactured in Japan, and companies such as Toyota and Honda were making the lion's share of the auto profits. North American auto manufacturers were the losers in that revolution, though ultimately it was a big win for consumers. The failure to quickly respond to that revolution nearly put the largest automakers in the world out of business.

Revolutions are funny things because we often don't know how important they are until we've been left behind by them. Imagine the first humans who settled down to grow crops instead of continuing to live as hunters and gatherers. It's unlikely that anyone at that time foresaw the radical change that was occurring and how it would affect human society: a decrease in infant mortality rates, exponential population growth, increased levels of organized violence, the birth of new primitive technologies, the promulgation of written language and communication, and in general a new way of life, from top to bottom.

The same is true of business revolutions. When Japanese cars were considered "cheap imports" in North America, no one suspected that the quality revolution would put companies like General Motors (GM) and Chrysler against the ropes. Remember the video store Blockbuster? It passed on an opportunity to purchase Netflix in part because its leaders didn't understand, or were unwilling to believe, the level of disruption that was about to take place in accessing and watching movies at home. Business revolutions spell death for some companies, but they also provide a climate in which other companies grow and thrive.

Human beings also have a strong tendency to underestimate rates of change. Most of the time, we get the general direction correct but we aren't ready for how rapidly a trend takes off once the trajectory is set.

Take the adoption of cell phones. In 1980 AT&T commissioned a study to estimate cell phone usage by the year 2000, concluding that there would be 900,000 cell phone users by that time.[20] By 2000 there were 109 million cell phone connections—120 times greater than estimated. Today there are 7.6 billion mobile subscriptions globally, with the number of subscriptions exceeding the population in some countries.[21]

Green energy provides another example of our tendency to underestimate adoption curves. In 2000 it was estimated that by 2010 worldwide electricity generated by wind would be 30 gigawatts. Come 2014, that figure was exceeded by 120 times. We see comparable trends and predictions in solar energy, as well. In 2012 the US Energy Information Administration reported that solar was projected to reach 24 gigawatts of capacity by 2035. During the first three months of 2017, the Federal Energy Regulatory Commission stated that utility-scale solar was already at 25.84 gigawatts, which doesn't even include small-scale systems such as rooftop solar.[22]

Similar stories can be told, from predictions of the growth of the automobile after the release of Ford's Model T to how many personal computers would be in use today. The commonality among all of these predictive misses is that we typically think of change as linear when it tends to be geometric. As Malcolm Gladwell profoundly showed in his book *The Tipping Point: How Little Things Can Make a Big Difference,* social phenomena start slowly at first, but when they reach the point of acceleration they take off. It is somewhat like a rocket ship slowly lifting off its launch platform but soon accelerating at rapid speed.

Purpose Can Make You Relevant in an Age of Disruption

Among the biggest changes in business over the past 15 years are both the rate of disruption as well as the commoditization of almost everything. Almost any business model can be disrupted and quite quickly. Think of what ride sharing has done to the taxi business and what "robo advisers" may soon do to financial planners. Alongside the potential for disruption is a relentless focus on price, where customers often desert brands in favor of less expensive alternatives. All of this raises the question: *Where does customer and employee loyalty come from when disruption is the norm and almost everything becomes a commodity?*

We think that connecting people to your purpose may potentially be one of the few sustainable competitive advantages available to businesses. As we show in this book, when customers connect to your purpose they are more loyal, even when your competitors cut prices; employees will stay and work hard, even when you face disruption; and your existing customers, as well as employees, will be enthusiastic ambassadors for your brand.

CLOSING THE PURPOSE GAP: LEADING IN AN AGE OF SOCIAL GOOD

Most leaders sense that purpose and social good are becoming critical drivers of business success, yet most companies are failing at purpose. Their efforts to close the gap posed by the emerging values and desires of the global population are simply insufficient. The purpose gap may be a threat to some companies, but it is a tremendous opportunity for others. Those companies and leaders who truly bridge the divide will become the purpose icons of our generation, in much the same way that Honda, Nordstrom, Southwest Airlines, and FedEx became the icons of the service quality revolution. Addressing the gap between what talent and customers want and how most companies are currently perceived will prove to be the most imperative business challenge of the twenty-first century.

Sustainable Brands is the leading community of interest on this issue. For more than 10 years, the company has been conducting conferences around the world, focused on how companies can prosper by creating brands with purpose. The company's founder and CEO, KoAnn Vikoren Skrzyniarz, told us that the window is going to close for companies that want to truly differentiate just by focusing on purpose: "There will always be opportunities for companies to go deeper; but if you want to differentiate just by having a purpose, it will soon be too late. Once having purpose is the lowest common denominator, you'll have to work a good deal harder."

The real question is whether your company will close the gap or be swallowed up by it. Will you personally be a leader who fosters a highly engaged, purpose-driven team? The chapters that follow provide an in-depth guide to thriving in the age of social good. Some readers may find that their companies' practices have already positioned their organizations well, but likely many more will find that they are woefully behind the purpose curve. Fear not; we're here to help you navigate this new world. Let's begin!

Harnessing the Power of Purpose

The core argument of this book is that there is a revolution of expectations happening among employees, customers, and investors that represents one of the biggest opportunities in our generation for engaging those stakeholders. The focus of part one is to help you understand what the purpose revolution is all about and why it matters to your enterprise and to you as a leader. We want you to really understand how your stakeholders define *purpose* and how the desire for meaning at work and for our actions to perpetuate social good are key to leveraging both engagement and loyalty for talent and customers in the age of social good.

This part will help you as a leader understand what purpose is, see how expectations are shifting, discover the business advantage of purpose, learn how to define your company's and team's purpose, and find out how to close what we call the *purpose gap*. You will also discover why most leaders and companies are currently failing at purpose and how to avoid the most common mistakes when it comes to engaging the emerging employee and customer.

CHAPTER 1

The Purpose Advantage

THERE IS LITTLE DOUBT THAT COMPANIES FOCUSED MORE DEEPLY on purpose and social good will be positive for their employees and for society at large. But does purpose create a meaningful competitive advantage for *your* enterprise? Few may disagree with the direction of the trends discussed in this book, but many may doubt whether it is the kind of game-changing force—the revolution—that we believe it to be. If you're thinking along these lines or asking yourself similar questions, we understand—you're not alone.

Many of the CEOs and leaders we interviewed, whose companies are already reaping significant benefit from a focus on purpose, suggested that *most* leaders still don't get how important this movement has already become. Inge Thulin, president, CEO, and chairman of 3M, for example, told us that "an enterprise not focused on sustainability for their own products and those of their customers will not exist in 50 years." Sustainability of course is bigger than just environment, though "being green" consistently tops the societal concerns of talent and consumers alike; it's about that aspirational focus on making things better.

Darren Entwistle, CEO of TELUS, a large, profitable Canadian telecommunications company and a leader in this revolution, is not only convinced that purpose is critical for business success but bluntly adds, "The vast majority of my CEO peers simply don't get the potential of moving in this direction."

We don't want to scare you into supporting the purpose-driven company philosophy discussed throughout this book, but we do want to show you that the facts all point to a changing world—an age of social good in which purpose increasingly lies at the heart of employee, customer, and investor motivation. We believe that once you understand the facts and the power of the purpose revolution, you won't be able to ignore it any longer. To start, let's consider the business case for purpose. There are three dimensions to explore: the risks of not focusing on purpose, the direct opportunity that comes from purpose, and the indirect benefits that derive from a purpose-driven culture.

THE BUSINESS CASE FOR PURPOSE

In the age of social good, there is great risk in not being a purpose-driven company that perpetuates social good. Take Volkswagen (VW), the German auto manufacturer whose scandal involving manipulating the software on its cars to deceive regulators about the vehicles' emissions cost the company billions of dollars in lawsuits and reparations to dealers, as well as customers. It also started a conversation among the car-buying public. A colleague told us recently about a conversation he had with a group of fellow professionals at a party, half of whom said they would never again buy a VW product. The value of VW stock has been decimated—cut in half—and there is a good chance the scandal will follow the company for years to come.

Many top talent, especially young recruits, now compile lists of companies they simply won't work for. Take the case of Lisa, a top grad from the Wharton School of the University of Pennsylvania, who told us, "My friends and I researched companies we felt were working against values we care about. Companies like Exxon[Mobil], VW, BP [British Petroleum], Monsanto, and about 30 others were on our list. We called it the 'no fly' list." Companies made the list for reasons ranging from environmental damage to ethical lapses.

Recruiters at 3M, Ford, and many other companies tell us that on college campuses, students increasingly come armed with information about the company's corporate reputation already in hand. One HR exec said to us, "They already know our story; they just want to know if it's real." If recruits believe that your company is serious about its mission, they'll be more open to working with you. If they find that there are holes in your corporate reputation, they won't mind writing you off—there are plenty of other companies out there whose values align with theirs.

Though the risk side is a strong case for purpose, the upside of being purpose driven is even stronger. Consider a 2015 study by IO Sustainability and Babson College titled *Project ROI Report: Defining the Competitive and Financial Advantages of Corporate Social Responsibility and Sustainability.*[1] The research study took a wide path to examine far-reaching data points and do a meta-analysis of whether being good pays off. The report found that "strong corporate responsibility (CR), which is one important part of the purpose equation, increases commitment, affinity, and engagement of employees." Note that *corporate social responsibility* is not synonymous with *purpose,* though it does play a role in how companies drive and activate purpose today.

The study reports that employees would be willing to take a 5 percent pay cut to work for an employer that is committed to social responsibility. Organizations with effective CR programs and approaches can increase productivity by up to 13 percent and reduce the annual quit rate by 3 to 3.5 percent, saving replacement costs of up to 90 to 200 percent of an employee's annual salary for each employee who stays. Over time the average turnover rate can be reduced by 25 to 50 percent.

The study also revealed that strong CR has a meaningful impact on marketing and sales and can "increase revenue by 20 percent; increase price premium up to 20 percent; and increase customer commitment in the total segment of 60 percent." Maybe most telling is that, according to Project ROI, corporate responsibility has the potential to "increase market value by up to 4–6 percent; over a 15-year period increase shareholder value by USD $1.28 billion; and avoid market losses from crisis by USD $378 million."

As you can see, we're not talking about chump change here; this is a phenomenon of epic proportions. If you don't heed the warning signs, you not only leave money on the table but also lose the best and brightest minds. This talent pool is not just domestic, either. One of the most important aspects of this revolution is that the purpose-centered employee is a global phenomenon cutting across borders. A 2016 global survey of 26,151 LinkedIn members in 40 different countries and speaking 16 different languages found that 37 percent of LinkedIn members are "purpose oriented" and "38 percent considered purpose to be equally weighted with either money or status."[2]

The countries rating highest on purpose orientation were Sweden (53 percent), Germany (50 percent), the Netherlands (50 percent), Belgium (49 percent), and Poland (48 percent). The United States showed a 40 percent purpose orientation in its workforce. The lowest purpose-oriented country in the study was Saudi Arabia, at 23 percent. For many companies the war for talent is a global fight, so showing how *your* team is helping solve the world's great challenges is becoming a ticket to engaging talent everywhere a company operates. And it's not just potential employees—it's potential new *customers*.

A GLOBAL OPPORTUNITY

One of the greatest opportunities in business today is in reaching the emerging global middle class. What it takes to win this growing market might surprise you. The rise of the middle class in the developing world, particularly in Asia, is a major aspect driving the purpose revolution. China, for example, has brought more people into the middle class and out of poverty in a shorter span of time than any society in human history. The Edelman Goodpurpose Study showed that 80 percent of consumers in China and 71 percent in India were willing to pay more for products from companies with a purpose.[3]

John Edwin Mroz, founder, president, and CEO of the EastWest Institute and a mentor of ours, spent a great deal of time working at high levels with the Chinese government. Behind the scenes their most senior people told him they were surprised that once they brought so many people into the middle class, expectations changed rapidly. Suddenly, people were demanding a clean environment and more accountability while increasing pressure on the government to address such specific issues as air pollution and food safety.

People in poverty don't generally push businesses to be more responsible, nor do they focus primarily on the sense of purpose they get at work; but once people rise to a higher income level, they begin considering these factors. Right now this is occurring across the developing world in greater numbers than ever before. This rising middle class in the developing world will pressure companies to take purpose and social responsibility very seriously.

In a 2015 *Forbes* article, Bill Fischer points out that the rising Chinese middle class and "growing focus on serving Chinese consumers" is driving companies to shift their culture toward innovation and that the most successful innovations are driven by "pursuing a sense of purpose."[4] One example of this is Shinho, a Chinese food company which, in the words of Charles Hayes, managing director of IDEO China, is motivated "not just by commercial objectives, but by using their business to improve people's lives."

Shinho's higher aspirations are evident in its mission: *We lead the diet to improve the ecology, so that family peace of mind to enjoy every meal, live music every day.*[5] Shinho's purpose is realized through its commitment to seven causes: sustainable agricultural cultivation, a reliable diet supply chain, innovative product development, high standards of manufacturing, convenient retail channels, an extreme diet experience, and a full range of food education.

As incomes rise internationally, an emerging desire for meaning is accompanied by disillusionment with modern life. Otto Scharmer, a senior lecturer at the Massachusetts Institute of Technology (MIT), refers to this idea as the "three divides of modern society": the nature divide, the social divide, and the spiritual divide. The nature divide is a growing disconnect between global society and our impact on the environment, evidenced most powerfully by the climate change crisis. The social divide is the increasing gap between rich and poor. The spiritual divide is the growing experience of loss of meaning often related to the experience at work.

These growing divides are fueling a wall of energy heading toward contemporary companies worldwide that will pressure them to address all three divides. Companies will soon be scrambling to keep pace with the emerging desires of talent and customers. Those companies perceived as proactively leading for change will become the preferred brands and employers.

THE COMPETITIVE ADVANTAGE STARTS WITH A CLEAR PURPOSE

In the coming chapters, we profile numerous leaders and companies that we believe are in the forefront of the purpose revolution, driving purpose within their organizations and teams while creating a better world in the process. As you'll see, some of these companies began with a clear purpose woven into the very product they make or service they provide. Others developed their purpose over time, finding what connects with their core values as people and as an organization, and how that relates to their employees and customers. Because unearthing that purpose and communicating it widely is a main tenant of engaging in the purpose revolution, the first step in activating purpose in *your* organization is to articulate a clear, compelling purpose, one that is bigger than simply making money.

To illustrate the potential of purpose to drive business advantage, take the case of Seventh Generation, which has continuously gained customers in large part due to its willingness to clearly and concisely promote its purpose and then back up the words with deeds.

Seventh Generation: Walking the Walk

Founded in 1988 in Burlington, Vermont, Seventh Generation sells cleaning, personal care, and paper products and supplies, with an emphasis on corporate responsibility, sustainability, the environment, and consumer health. The company's mission is "to inspire a consumer revolution that nurtures the health of the next seven generations."[6]

The company's dish and hand soaps, diapers and wipes, botanical disinfectants, and feminine hygiene products are all made with the customer's best interests at heart, using biodegradable, recyclable, and organic materials and avoiding harmful or harsh chemicals and plastics. The company is particularly well known for its laundry detergent—and not just because it keeps people's clothes smelling fresh and clean.

Seventh Generation believes, as many of its customers do, that people should know what ingredients go into their cleaning products. Customers see the company's commitment to sustainability right on the labels, highlighting the key value attributes of its products. For example, on laundry detergent: "No dyes, optical brighteners or synthetic fragrances, Seventh Generation Laundry Detergent... [is] made with plant-based ingredients [and] is a USDA Certified Biobased Product 97%."[7] On the dishwasher detergent, in addition to no dyes or synthetic fragrances, the label communicates: "Chlorine bleach and phosphate free."[8] In fact, the company believes so strongly in customer education on this issue that it has taken significant steps toward ingredient transparency for all cleaning-product companies.

The case of a campaign the company ran shows how being purpose driven is good business. In 2014 Seventh Generation led an effort tied to Earth Day aimed at getting the US Congress to pass a bill focused on toxic chemical safety reform, asking people to demand greater regulation over chemical safety. The company ran a full-page ad in the *New York Times*, asking citizens for 100,000 signatures on a petition to get the bill passed. The ad focused on why the issue mattered for the planet and for society—and it didn't mention the company's products.

Joey Bergstein, Seventh Generation's CEO, says that the ad had a larger impact on sales volume than did all the coupons they offered for a year—even though those directly benefit the customer's wallet. The company tackled an issue that it felt was important to its customers and invited them to get involved directly. The campaign was much more than a simple marketing effort. It solidified Seventh Generation's relationships with its customers and reinforced its mission for good.

The company's current campaign focuses on ingredient disclosure—the Cleaning Product Right to Know Act. The campaign invites people to join the effort to make product labeling transparent and offers clear suggestions on what they can do: "Make sure you're only using products that list their ingredients on the labels" and "Support the Cleaning Product Right to Know Act (H.R. 2728) by contacting your US representative."[9]

Seventh Generation regularly demonstrates its values and shows that it has skin in the game, inviting its growing customer base to participate when it takes a stand. By showing its customers that they are in this fight together and that its actions align with its customers' needs and principles, the company is already winning the purpose advantage.

While this ad campaign was a genuine expression of Seventh Generation's purpose, it also serves as an example to any organization that wants to close the purpose gap and help consumers make the "good" choices they want to make.

Because we never know what will resonate with customers, it's critical to test your purpose initiatives for business impact. Rather than traditional marketing, such testing is ultimately about building a more authentic relationship with consumers centered around your shared values.

EXERCISE   *How Would Your Organization Score on Purpose?*

For this first exercise, we want to get you thinking about purpose in your organization and how you think it would score if tested. Jot down the answers to the following questions and refer back to them as you read subsequent chapters. Be specific in your responses.

- Do you know your company's purpose? What is it, and how does it relate to your work every day?

- How often do you discuss concepts like purpose or values in formal meetings—or even in informal conversations with peers and colleagues?

- Based on what you're read so far, do you believe that your company is ahead of the purpose revolution, in line with it, or falling behind it?

- What issues in your company do you see as roadblocks to driving purpose?

- Who owns purpose in the company? The CEO? Leaders? All employees? You?

CHAMPION A CAUSE

Developing a clear purpose isn't always easy. We've heard from numerous leaders who believe that their company is already too established or traditional—or that the product they sell doesn't lend itself to a purpose like Seventh Generation's—to enable a purpose that will strongly resonate with customers and employees. Sure, Seventh Generation's purpose is essentially laid out in its name, but there are many other companies that are leading with purpose and, in so doing, are attracting and retaining top talent and customers.

The way they do this is by championing a cause that aligns with their customers', employees', and other stakeholders' values, beliefs, or ethics. When your company stands for more than a great product or service, you effect a qualitative shift in the relationship between your company and others. The product or service relationship is transcended, as the company is now viewed as a community member, a valued partner in a group assembled around a common good. Many companies avoid taking a stand to avoid the risk of alienating or turning away potential customers, but people tend to respect companies with the courage to try to right the wrongs that they see in the world.

Championing a cause that you believe in provides hope and builds trust, not just in your company but in business overall. For those companies clear about their own purpose, clear about their customers' values, and clear about their commitment to doing the right thing first, their actions become a way of life—and they need not always be grandiose gestures. Taking a stand can be as simple as sending a clear message during times of uncertainty.

TAKE A STAND

Amid the confusion and emotion over the 2017 Muslim travel ban and talk about building a wall on the US-Mexico border, Anheuser-Busch supported immigration when it ran its Budweiser commercial during the Super Bowl. The portrayal of its cofounder Adolphus Busch, a German immigrant, shows him rising above obstacles and the prejudices of his day to create a great American company. Honoring its own legacy, Anheuser-Busch spoke out against the idea that immigrants are a dangerous lot or that they are coming to the United States to sponge off the system. Rather, the commercial portrayed immigrants as the heart of the entrepreneurial spirit still alive in the country, the true foundation of the American dream.

Howard Schultz, executive chairman and former CEO of Starbucks, also took a public stance on the immigration issue. In response to the Muslim travel ban, he tweeted, "We are living in an unprecedented time, one in which we are witness to the conscience of our country, and the promise of the American Dream, being called into question." Despite some calls for boycotting Starbucks by supporters of the travel ban, Schultz stood by his convictions. As reported by TheStreet.com, he announced that "Starbucks is developing plans to hire 10,000 refugees over the next five years across the 75 countries globally where it does business," and he renewed the company's commitment to working with Mexico, which is a large source of the coffee maker's beans."[10]

Leveraging social media like Schultz or mainstream media like Anheuser-Busch are clear, effective ways to champion a cause and work toward a better world. Anheuser-Busch's reliance on the company's heritage and immigrant and entrepreneurial roots spoke volumes. Building on a company's traditions can go a long way.

EXERCISE   *The Strength of Heritage*

Consider the following questions to see how you can help activate purpose in your team by looking to your company's heritage for inspiration.

- What were the values and aspirations of the company founders?

- What good did they promote beyond profit alone?

- What was their vision for a better world?

- What causes did they stand for or support in their day?

- What's your company's story of good today, how do you stay true to that story, and what chapter will you add going forward?

As you explore ways to activate your company's purpose, consider real-time opportunities to express your beliefs and purpose. When you look around, what are the pressing issues? What's in the news? Where is the debate? Is your company in the game or on the sidelines? Take initiative, strike while the iron is hot on key issues of the day, and send a clear message about where your company stands.

YOUR PEOPLE ARE HUNGRY FOR PURPOSE

As you consider the global implications of the purpose revolution, you may think of this trend as one that is happening *to* your business when in fact it is already taking place *within* your business. Most of us want our work to have purpose—to serve something greater than profits—and we want our legacy to leave a better world for those who come after us, let alone for those of us already here.

The fact that this desire already exists among most employees and customers means we have tremendous assets to draw on as we move in this direction. Rather than having to ignite your company around purpose, the main goal is to harness what is already there.

For example, Canadian National Railway Company (CN), a major rail transport company based in Montreal, set lofty goals to reduce its carbon footprint while also reducing waste and energy use. When Chantale Després, director of sustainability for CN, began her career in sales and marketing, she was intrigued by the emerging trend of customers asking questions about environmental issues. She is herself an example of the many people we have met who have seen their own work satisfaction skyrocket as they navigated to positions within their company where they feel they can make a difference on issues affecting society.

In our discussions with Després, she told us, "As we began our efforts toward becoming greener, we really wanted to find a way to do it from the bottom up. Before we started we surveyed our employee base and found tremendous support for our doing this. We wanted to find a way that every team member could feel part of what we were trying to accomplish." They created a program called EcoConnexions, a ground-up effort to get people from all over the company more engaged by involving them in attempts to reduce waste and increase efficiency.

Across the company leaders asked employees to step up to become "sustainability EcoChampions" in each of the company's railyards throughout North America. The response was overwhelmingly positive. As they rolled out the program to their more than 120 locations, there were often many more people who wanted to be the local EcoChampion than there were positions. "We discovered there were a great many 'closet' champions for the environment already out there, and this gave them a way to bring that passion to their work and become program leaders. Not only have we made great progress on reducing our carbon footprint and diverting waste but we find that many newer employees are very interested in what we are doing." The EcoConnexions program is focused not just on the leaders in each yard but on every person stepping up every day to look for ways to become greener and more efficient.

The point is we don't have to look outside of our business to find this purpose revolution; it is already happening within our business. Each of us as a leader has likely had our own moments when we feel that the place we work is out of alignment with the purpose we have in our life.

A few years ago, an executive working for one of our clients talked to us about the consistent disconnect she felt between her values and her daily work. She mentioned that every week she was asked to make decisions in her role as an executive that were against her personal values. She dreaded coming into work week after week, knowing that she'd have to make a call on issues she just couldn't get behind. She questioned her own values as a leader and as an employee and knew that her work didn't match the high standards she held for herself and the company. She felt she could not express those feelings to her colleagues; there simply wasn't a place for a purpose conversation. Eventually, she left that job for an organization that she felt was purpose driven, robbing the former company of one of its best performers.

Have you ever felt that way as a leader? What was the impact on your commitment, engagement, and ultimate willingness to work hard for the company? This kind of disconnect is corrosive in any organization and ultimately means we won't get the best from our people. This disconnect can happen as easily in nonprofit organizations like health care as it can in for-profit companies when employees experience a disconnect between the organization's stated purpose and values and how decisions are made day to day. By leaning into the deeper desire for purpose that already exists in our companies, we can energize people toward success.

Heineken Mexico: Not Just Selling Suds

In looking for companies that exemplify where the purpose revolution is headed, we think Heineken Mexico hits all the checkmarks discussed in this chapter. A global company whose primary consumers are part of an emerging middle class, Heineken Mexico has developed a competitive advantage by getting clear on purpose, activating it within the company, championing a cause, and in the process connecting with employees, customers, and the community in new ways.

When Dolf van den Brink moved to Mexico from the United States in 2015, he saw a country with great potential but also many challenges. As the new CEO of Heineken Mexico—the largest national division for the company worldwide—he understood that one of Heineken's purposes was to "win big" by growing its brands, but he also sensed the opportunity for so much more. The company had a long history of service in Mexico, including starting one of the most respected universities in Monterrey and offering health care to employees and their families in the days when few companies did so. Van den Brink wanted to seize the chance to emphasize Heineken Mexico's commitment to its employees, customers, and maybe—above all—the community at large.

His own experiences working in the Congo connected him to the real difference that companies can make in the communities in which they live and operate. His quest to redefine the purpose of Heineken Mexico began by getting his senior leaders to look at their own personal values. What was their personal purpose in life? What were they trying to create?

"People have this idea of what business is about that is often disconnected from their own personal purpose," van den Brink says. "If you want leaders to discover purpose, it has to begin as a personal question. I find that when you get people talking about the business, they focus on profits; but when you first get people thinking about their personal purpose, what they want to be true in their personal lives, this is where the true magic happens—because the purpose of most people's life is not simply to make money."

Through this process that began by examining personal purpose, van den Brink's team ultimately connected to the idea that the company could "help Mexico fulfill its highest potential." In part that realization led to a new purpose statement: *To win big for a better Mexico.*

One of the first initiatives to activate this new purpose was bold. Violence against women in Mexico is a major problem and often widely accepted as a fact of life. According to one study, 63 percent of Mexican women over 15 years old have experienced some form of gender violence, which could include physical, sexual, emotional, or psychological violence.[11] In 2015 BBC News reported that in Mexico a woman is raped every four minutes.[12]

One of Heineken Mexico's brands, Tecate, is considered a premiere "man's beer," historically associated with ads and calendars replete with attractive, half-dressed women. The company decided to confront violence against women and help redefine a new masculinity as part of the larger purpose of a better Mexico.

To start, they ran a bold television ad about violence against women that ends by saying, "If you're a man who is abusive to women, *you aren't one of us—don't buy our beer.*" It was honest, blunt, and a bit of a risk. When was the last time you saw an ad from a brand, saying, "Don't buy our product?" But the ad and the subsequent social media campaign left little doubt that Heineken was serious about winning big for a better Mexico. Later that year they ran ads about *"no" meaning no* as part of the overall goal to offer up a new version of masculinity. The response within the company in terms of activating purpose and showing that Heineken was serious about a "better Mexico" was overwhelmingly positive.

Heineken Mexico's social awareness and support of its community, spurred on under van den Brink's leadership, exhibits a company embracing the global purpose revolution. The underlying values connect with employees, consumers, and other stakeholders—including shareholders.

Mexico is one of the fastest-growing markets for Heineken globally. To respond to that momentum in recent years, the company announced a significant investment program to accelerate capacity expansions. It's been reported that Heineken Mexico may need to add production capacity to its operation by the end of 2017.[13] Parent company Heineken also cited the Latin American market and double-digit revenue growth of Sol, its Mexican light beer, as major contributors to its 2016 revenue growth of 3.5 percent, operating profits of 6.9 percent, and net profits of 16 percent.[14]

While the jury is still out on the business impact of this new, more purpose-focused direction, the fact that companies like Heineken Mexico are focusing on trying to influence the social fabric in positive ways speaks volumes about what the future holds. We believe that in the purpose revolution those willing to boldly take a stand will be rewarded. If your purpose is real, it will resonate.

BEST PRACTICES FOR
INITIATING THE PURPOSE ADVANTAGE

- Honestly assess where your company stands regarding purpose and how well it is positioned for the purpose revolution. Can you easily identify your company's purpose and how it is being approached and activated?

- Consider your business case for purpose. Can you and other leaders clearly articulate your company's purpose and how it makes a difference to your customers and society?

- Research other companies in your industry to see how they are approaching the purpose revolution. What is the conversation around purpose at conferences, meetings, and industry-related events?

- Read up on companies driving purpose in other industries as well, especially those that are global in nature.

- Think about your personal values and how you are personally contributing to purpose in your organization. Do you see your personal values come to life at work? Even if you are not a senior leader, how are you driving purpose in your team or area of responsibility?

- If your company hasn't yet identified its true purpose, consider how its actions, products, or services can make a difference in society, directly or indirectly.

- Uncover the aspirational purpose of your business. What do you think it is, even if it doesn't have credibility yet in the larger organization?

- Build on the strength of your company's heritage. Discuss your company's story, its founders, and ways you can add to the story.

- Look for opportunities to champion a cause in your community.

CHAPTER 2

First, Find Your Purpose

@ 1: 24: 05

THE FIRST STEP THAT EVERY LEADER, ORGANIZATION, AND COMPANY must take to thrive in the age of social good is to clearly find and name your purpose. Once you have named it, your job is to move it to center stage. By that we mean you must *live* the purpose you profess: having a purpose is not enough if it is not what truly drives your business. If companies want to close the purpose gap, their leaders can't be afraid to be open and honest about their approach to purpose. They should feel free to claim a moral mandate—a justification for and pride in the purpose-oriented actions that not only positively influence company performance but also have a meaningful impact on the world.

We need to get over whatever fear we have of saying that we care about the present and future good of our customers as well as society and actively move purpose to the center of our business. Companies need to start by discovering the real purpose behind their work and activating it throughout the organization.

We often think of a CEO named Michael S. Eesley, who in 1999 took over two hospitals in rural northwestern Illinois called Centegra Health System. At the time the hospitals had mediocre patient satisfaction and clinical quality, as well as relatively low engagement. Led by the new CEO, the board came up with a powerful vision: *To be a destination hospital in the Midwest with the clinical quality of the Mayo*

Clinic and the service reputation of the Ritz-Carlton. This vision of greatness was almost laughable, given the hospitals' historical performance on both fronts.

Eesley could have pursued both those aims as a good business strategy, which surely it was. Raising patient satisfaction and clinical quality would result in more business for the hospitals, ensure greater job security for the employees, and bring distinction to Eesley himself. But having talked to Eesley and many of those who worked at Centegra during the critical early years of transformation, it was obvious that he deeply connected his people to a type of moral mandate around this purpose. Purpose was the center of the change, not on the edge.

The reason to pursue clinical quality like the Mayo Clinic was not because it was simply good business but because people in small, rural communities deserved just as good a chance for a healthy life—and to survive a heart attack and to receive high-quality care—as those who live a few blocks from Mayo. Service like the Ritz-Carlton wasn't just a good strategy to keep customers coming back or to raise Net Promoter Scores but was motivated by the belief that those who come to Centegra in the most vulnerable moments of their lives deserve to be treated with at least as much dignity as they would at an excellent five-star hotel.

Over the ensuing decade, against the odds, Centegra transformed itself to become a regional leader in both clinical quality and patient satisfaction. The health system won awards for excellent service and became a Top 100 Hospital in several clinical areas (a distinction quite rare for a rural hospital system in the United States); it moved into the top 1 percent of hospitals in patient satisfaction, and staff engagement skyrocketed. Business success followed, but it was defining a clear purpose and moving purpose to the center—the real difference they could make in the lives of patients and the community—that were in the driver's seat.

EVERY COMPANY HAS TWO PURPOSES

One of the critical questions for us as leaders to ask is *How do our team members and customers define purpose?* We believe that when it comes to purpose, there are really *two* elements that matter and must be activated. You might think of them as two purposes or two sides of the purpose coin. The first is the basic relationship we have with our customers. Do we really care about their well-being as much or more than we do our profits? The second purpose is to society—to help society solve its key problems, including promoting a more sustainable planet. It turns out that our employees care deeply about both of those purposes, so we better make sure we are activating both.

Each year the professional services group Deloitte conducts a survey on an array of topics to shed light on current trends, changes, and issues in the economy and the business world. In its 2014 *Culture of Purpose* study, Deloitte found that focusing on purpose over profits "builds business confidence and drives investment."[1] One issue they were particularly concerned with was how employees define and understand purpose. When asked what makes a company "purpose driven," employees were most likely to cite the positive impact that products and services have on customers (89 percent) and the impact the company has on society (84 percent). In other words, employees say that both customers and society overall matter to them but that the basic relationship companies have with customers matters a little more.

The fact that your customer is your primary purpose makes sense. Basically, businesses can't exist without their customers; and without businesses, customers would lose out on all the wonderful products and services that improve their lives. Companies leading with purpose form a deeper relationship with customers beyond the transactional level of buying and selling. They know their customers' values, what's important to them, who they are, what they believe in, what they stand for, and what they expect and need from the company's brand. Rather than focus on *selling* to the customer, companies that thrive in the purpose revolution focus on *connecting* with the customer.

Your second purpose is the world—how your company is an agent for good in the greater society. Purpose-driven companies recognize that they are meaningful members of the global community, not external agencies void of influence or impact. They make a deliberate choice to understand and lean into the problems and issues facing the world, exhibiting the courage to take a stand and champion causes they believe in. Real action—dedicating time, energy, and resources to important causes—makes purpose come alive.

Of course, the two sides of the purpose coin are not mutually exclusive. If the purpose revolution has taught us anything so far, it's that when companies infuse themselves with purpose, they affect *all* stakeholders—direct ones, such as customers, and indirect ones, such as the community in which the company operates. This idea pans out on a global level: doing good by customers does good for the world and vice versa. By first connecting to the needs and desires of the customer, your company can start making a significant direct impact. Today it's your customers; tomorrow it's the world. Lose sight of either, however, at your peril.

Wells Fargo: Failing at the Prime Directive

It could easily be argued that when it comes to purpose, doing right for your customers is every company's prime directive. Recall that more than 70 percent of employees say that the company they work for is more interested in its own needs than the well-being of its customers. When we fail to live up to that core purpose, it spells real trouble.

In 2016 Wells Fargo & Company experienced a public relations nightmare when it was discovered that employees had opened accounts in customers' names without their consent. As the scandal unfolded, the company's stock price plummeted and stories of unethical pressure on employees to open new accounts came to light. While the crisis was indeed a public scandal, it was also deeply felt *within* the company as an internal challenge to the sense of purpose for those who worked there.

Two midlevel leaders at Wells Fargo told us how disillusioned they were and how this was "not the bank we thought we were part of." One of them told us, "Now when I am out somewhere, I have to sheepishly tell people that I work for Wells Fargo, when I used to say it loud and proud." They went on to explain how they'd always felt that the company held the interests of its clients as its top priority, and they fervently hoped that the debacle was the result of the work of just a small group of rogue leaders.

This would turn out not to be the case. It was revealed that more than 2 million fake accounts were opened without customers' permission. Furthermore, the practice was deep-seated: it started in 2011, and in the end more than 5,300 employees were fired for creating those bogus accounts.² Apparently, Wells Fargo executives were aware of the problem, and due to pressure from shareholders and US politicians, chairman and CEO John Stumpf retired in the middle of the scandal.

Wells Fargo lost sight of its vision to put customers first and help them succeed financially.³ Though the company aimed to build lasting relationships "one customer at a time," it failed to meet the most basic and fundamental goal of any business: to serve the best interests of its customers always. In the process, the company also failed its second purpose—its commitment to the broader society. Considering the enormous role that banks play in the world economy, their actions have major consequences. Wells Fargo failed not just its own customers but consumers across the banking industry.

Show You Really Care

Unlike Wells Fargo, when a company connects the well-being of its customers with social responsibility, a deep sense of purpose takes root in the organization. A powerful example is The Vanguard Group, a rather humble company that has grown to be the largest mutual fund manager in the world and, given current growth rates, may soon surpass BlackRock to become the largest money manager on the planet. Vanguard began with a simple, powerful purpose: to take a stand for all investors, to treat them fairly, and to give them the best chance for investment success.

The company was founded by John C. Bogle, who believed that most investors were paying far too much for mutual funds that were underperforming the overall market. He set out not only to educate investors but to create funds with expenses among the lowest available.

We first met Bogle in 1996, long before most people knew what Vanguard was. An hour-long conversation left us convinced that he was a man with a purpose, one focused not on making profits but on making a difference for people. Over the next 20 years, Vanguard quietly lived that purpose. Through financial crises and recessions, the company kept itself out of the headlines and set a bar for low-cost mutual and exchange funds that drove fees lower across the industry— all the while keeping investors' money safe. Interactions with Vanguard team members today quickly reveal the level of commitment such a purpose brings forth in talent, and Vanguard has among the lowest churn of investor money.

Another great example is Nissan's goal of zero fatalities, which focuses on building vehicles so safe that no one dies in a Nissan automobile. Nissan is also considered the industry leader in the manufacture of zero-emissions cars—but the company still places consumers first.[4] The company's simple corporate vision, *Enriching people's lives,* speaks directly to this fact.[5] Zero fatalities is a bold, inspiring expression of that purpose to enrich people's lives. A company can be in the forefront of electric cars that reduce emissions responsible for climate change—a commitment to its secondary purpose—but ensuring that people are safe in their vehicles fulfills the company's primary purpose: a commitment to its customers.

The essence of making the customer your primary purpose is summed up in one word: *relationship.* It is no longer a transaction that binds the brand to the customer but a relationship based on mutual values and causes. Companies leading with purpose form more-personal relations with their customers by developing interactive platforms, investing time and energy on mutual causes, and providing opportunities for customers to directly experience the company purpose. This movement is one from *us and them* to *we*, from what companies can get to what they can give, and what we—customers and companies—can accomplish together.

Raphael Bemporad, founding partner of BBMG, a top marketing firm in the purpose space, has experienced this shift firsthand and has been happy to embrace it as part of the purpose revolution. BBMG partners with some of the world's leading data miners to understand the emerging trends among consumers around the globe. Bemporad believes that for many years the business paradigm was essentially focused on "gimmicks" based on discounts and advertising, to almost "trick" people into buying. The best-in class purpose organizations, however, have "abandoned marketing and gimmicks in favor of relationship." Bemporad sees a sea change in terms of how companies connect with stakeholders, especially customers: "We are moving from the primacy of product to the primacy of relationship."

Until very recently, companies found relevance primarily from connecting people to their products and services, mostly a one-way transactional affair. We made products, we told customers about the benefits of those products, and then we tried to get them to buy those products. Muhtar Kent, chairman and former CEO of Coca-Cola, framed it this way: "In the old days, you made a good product, manufactured it with quality so that it tasted good, and then made it available. All you had to do was have the product be well understood through good advertising." Of course, good products still matter, as do all the other traditional differentiators, but true relevance now comes from connecting with customers' deepest values and the ability to build an authentic relationship.

START ACTIVATING PURPOSE

We have identified three ways in which the best companies and leaders discover and activate their higher purpose: they realize that their business *is* their cause, they fit purpose to their business, and they activate employees' personal purpose. No matter if you're a top-level executive or a new hire right out of college, this trifecta embeds purpose in every employee's actions and mind-set while contributing to a better world.

Your Business *Is* Your Cause

Though there are some exceptions, we believe that nearly every business has inherent purpose, that its products or services in and of themselves have the potential in some way to make the world a better place. Most organizational founders start off with a cause or with a need to fill or a high ideal in mind. They look to provide a solution to a problem—they have a mission. We have found that the best companies at leading purpose never stray from their mission; they focus inward on who they are, what they do, and where they are going. Knowing your business and staying true to the values it espouses is the starting point to framing your company's higher purpose.

For example, Bimbo Bakeries USA feeds people—a pretty noble start. Its mission and purpose is founded on traditional brands known for fresh products dating back to the 1800s and early 1900s. For Bimbo this is when "our traditions of freshness and value began." The company's mission statement is simply *Delicious and nutritious baked goods and snacks in the hands of all.* Note how this mission connects to a larger purpose as well, moving beyond baked goods as objects to a moral imperative larger than the product itself. The words *nutritious* and *in the hands of all* highlight the company's hope that its food will not only taste good but provide sustenance to the largest group of people possible. It then goes a step further in its purpose statement: *Building a sustainable, highly productive and deeply humane company.* In doing so Bimbo Bakeries connects with both employees and customers.

Is Purpose the Same as Mission?

Is a mission statement the same as a purpose? Although they can sometimes be one and the same, we think there is a meaningful difference. A *mission statement* explains what the company does, whereas a *purpose statement* describes why a company exists for the benefit of all stakeholders, now and in the future.

Recall the example of Heineken Mexico and the potential difference between *win big* and *win big for a better Mexico.* A company can have a mission simply to win, but that doesn't fit how the emerging talent and consumers define purpose. Though companies can have two distinct statements—one a mission statement, the other a purpose statement—we find that the most effective mission statements are effectively purpose statements, whether for a team or an entire organization. A great contrast, for example, can be found in comparing the mission statements of Adidas and Nike.

The Adidas Group strives to be the global leader in the sporting goods industry, building its brands on a passion for sports and a sporting lifestyle. Its mission statement reflects this idea: *We are committed to continuously strengthening our brands and products to improve our competitive position.* Though Nike has a similar mission, its mission statement includes a deeper purpose: *To bring inspiration and innovation to every athlete in the world.* (The legendary University of Oregon track and field coach and Nike cofounder, Bill Bowerman, said, "If you have a body, you are an athlete.") One statement inspires and stretches beyond the basic service provided and the company's bottom line.

Many mission statements are "purpose" statements, but in some cases there is a big difference in terms of fostering engagement in an age of social good—a core theme of the purpose revolution. This is not to say that Adidas is not driven by purpose, but the contrast in language helps us understand the subtle difference and why clear articulation of purpose matters.

A team can have a purpose just like a company can, so this work is important at whatever level you lead. Even if your company has a compelling purpose, it is critical that each leader and team define their purpose in terms of truly making things better for customers and society.

If your organization doesn't yet have a clear, compelling, well-articulated purpose, you can develop one for your team with positive results.

EXERCISE   *Developing a Company/Team Purpose Statement*

We regularly work with companies on defining their higher purpose, to help them build purpose into their mission state-ment or develop a separate purpose statement. We begin by having them ask themselves questions about their organi-zation and then look for patterns in their responses. To start thinking about your company's or team's higher purpose and how to create a purpose-driven mission statement, consider the following questions and write down your answers.

- Why does our company/team exist? What contribution do we make to our employees, customers, communi-ties, and the planet? How do we make the world a better place?

- What's our company's background? Why was the company started in the first place? Who are the founding members, and what was their mission and vision? What does our founding purpose and initial success tell us about who we really are as a company?

- What has been our journey, and what aspects of it have been critical to our success? What moments in history or what people really helped define our company?

Use your existing company purpose statement or, starting with the questions above, write a simple purpose state-ment; then evaluate the quality of your statement using the following criteria and rate it on a scale of 1 to 3—with 1 being *false,* 2 being *somewhat true,* and 3 being *true.*

Write your company's or team's purpose statement here:

_____

_____

_____

Statement quality assesment

_____ **Authentic.** It is genuine, true to who we are.

_____ **Compelling.** It sparks interest and moves people to stretch boundaries.

_____ **Congruent with what you really do.** It fits the nature of our business, mission, and values.

_____ **Scalable.** Employees at all levels of the organization can relate to it and make it their own.

_____ **Attainable.** It is realistic and doable.

_____ **Connects with the talent we want to attract and retain.** It fits with the interests and values of employees and recruits.

_____ **Connects with our customers.** It fits with the interests and values of our customers.

_____ **Connects with our investors.** It fits with the values of our investors.

_____ **Total score**

Scoring

Less than 16: Room for improvement

17–20: Good start

21–24: Excellent

Where did you score high? Low? Do this exercise with other leaders or your team. Compare scores and generate a group average. Discuss how to leverage higher scores and ways to improve the quality of your purpose so that you can have a purpose that matters!

Fit Purpose to Your Business

The key task for every company is to find a purpose that truly fits their unique business. Companies know they can't solve all of the world's problems, but they find a connection among their business, society, and the environment in which their purpose can emerge around common causes that they *can* influence. Purpose-centered companies are attuned to what they do best and offer their products, services, or expertise in support of higher causes.

The best companies know where they naturally fit when it comes to purpose and how they can leverage the products or services they provide to foster good in society, help the communities in which they operate, and keep the environment in mind. Take a moment to ask yourself: *Where do we fit? How can we use our business for social good? What do our communities need from us, and what can we provide for them? What is our impact on the environment?*

We see this in Coca-Cola, a company with a long history of sustainability, which has a deliberate approach to how its higher purpose plays out in society. For example, Coca-Cola does not make medicine, but after connecting with an aid worker via Facebook, the company found that it could use its supply-chain expertise to help in the distribution of medicines to improve health in the communities in which it operates.[6] Muhtar Kent, Coca-Cola's chairman and former CEO, understands the significance of this dialogue and its possibilities for social good: "Social media is a major driver of this new business model. When we get to a trillion tweets a day, the whole game will change and all businesses will need to pay attention to this."

After purpose-led organizations figure out how they fit into a cause or potential social change, a best practice is to distill their higher purpose into well-defined programs with clear targets, metrics, and mechanisms for reporting results internally and externally. For example, Coca-Cola—whose purpose statement is *To refresh the world in mind, body, and spirit. To inspire moments of optimism and happiness through our brands and actions*—clearly exhibits its purpose in its actions. Kent described Coca-Cola's social responsibility efforts in a recent article: "Sustainability isn't new to us but we've been intensifying our focus on it. We're prioritizing programs centered on water, women and well-being—all three of which are essential to our business."[7]

Looking at one of Coca-Cola's priorities, water, we see this practice in action. Focusing on water is a natural fit for a company whose prime product is a beverage that uses large amounts of water around the world. The company initiated a clearly defined water stewardship program that is built around three pillars—water efficiency, water replenishment, and wastewater—safely returning to the environment water that had been used in bottling.

The company established measurable goals, action plans, and annual reports for each water-related pillar, explained in detail on Coca-Cola's website. For example, the goal of the water efficiency program is: "By 2020, improve water efficiency in manufacturing operations by 25 percent compared with a 2010 baseline."[8] A recent check of the website shows that the water efficiency program is on track to meet its targets: "In 2016, we improved our water efficiency 2 percent. This is a total improvement of 13 percent since 2010 and 27 percent since 2004 when we started reporting efficiency progress as a global system."[9] This program is important for the community and aligns with Coca-Cola's business.

But what about this core idea of "refreshing the world"? Coca-Cola's drinks have always been refreshing, but the moments of optimism and happiness touted in its statement are not about its products. Instead they come from a purpose that can be accomplished in the process of providing those products. For employees and customers, this purpose is a fit for what the company makes and how they make it. We can debate the benefits and ills of sugar-based soft drinks, but ask anyone who regularly uses the product and they will tell you that for them it is refreshing.

So, purpose doesn't always have to please everyone, but it had better work for the core people you are trying to reach—and with an actual commitment to making the world better (such as the company's efforts on water) to pass the credibility test. At that point the refreshing happiness and optimism connects to a more emotional purpose that goes deeper than the product itself.

Smarter Planet: Now There's a Fit Purpose

Sometimes—and it sure is ideal when possible—a company can find a few words that perfectly express its purpose and how it serves its core business. IBM gives insight into developing that kind of purpose. The company's Smarter Planet vision aims to leverage new technologies and intelligent systems to enable "smarter power grids, smarter food systems, smarter water, smarter health care, [and] smarter traffic systems."[10] For example, the company's Smarter Cities initiative aims to develop greener, more vibrant cities.

Smarter Planet began as a strategy, but over time it began to feel more like the core of what the company was about: developing innovative solutions to major world problems. As Jen Crozier, vice president of corporate citizenship and president of the IBM Foundation, told us, "It really aligned with what we were doing—the energy we were feeling from our clients and how we could address social issues. It resonated beyond what we had imagined even more than we thought it would." One result of the program is Big Blue—IBM's supercomputer that is now exploring how to use information to enable better medicine through knowledge integration.

Smarter Planet works because it focuses on IBM's primary offer to the world. Since the company long ago left behind its emphasis on home computers and hardware solutions, it has refocused on harnessing knowledge and innovation to solve the world's most pressing issues. It is now just as easy for IBM to manage data for business success as it is to manage large applications like Big Blue. Crozier has been at the company for almost 20 years, and she had a front-row seat to the way the Smarter Planet strategy energized the company.

"It really began to energize IBM'ers, and at one point," she told us, "employees began creating their own videos about what they were doing at IBM and how they were personally contributing to a smarter planet. Then we started hearing stories of how this was also making a difference for clients and communities. The media picked it up, and eventually people were literally beating down the doors, wanting to come work for us."

You get the picture.

EXERCISE   *Decide Where Your Company Fits*

Companies like Coca-Cola and IBM have identified how they can do the most good based on their strengths, products, services, and even infrastructure. Both are major corporations with huge staffs and access to immense resources, but the idea behind their actions can be applied to a business of any size. Whether you are part of a start-up or a Fortune 500 company, ask yourself the following questions to figure out how to best fit purpose to your organization.

- Who buys your products, uses your services, and wants to work for you?

- Who are your customers, employees, and investors?

  - What do they expect and need from you? What do they care about? How does your purpose reflect their values and causes?

  - How well do you understand their hopes and aspirations for society and the planet? What kind of world do they want?

- How do you source, build, and deliver your products or services? How does that process fit with the values of your customers, employees, and investors?

- What communities do you serve?

  - What needs, problems, and challenges exist in your community? How can you play a role and make a difference?

  - Whom can you partner with? Who else has a vested interest in the well-being of the communities and environments in which you operate?

Your answers will help you gain clarity and understanding around your business's purpose. We find that many people have never stopped to consider these questions, but when they do they are able to look at both their company's role in the greater good and their own personal contributions. Once they discover the true impact they can make, they even see their job and organization in a different, more positive light. Realizing that you can be an agent of change—no matter where you work—brings fulfillment and excitement, influencing others around you and improving business results.

Discovering Your Personal Purpose

The third way that companies discover and activate their purpose is by helping employees activate their own *personal* purpose at work. We know that employees look to their jobs as a place to find meaning. Connecting your company's higher purpose to day-to-day work is one way to accomplish this. We have found, however, that companies that are best at leading with purpose add something extra: they have a clear focus on their higher purpose, but they leave room for people to find themselves and to discover their own personal purpose, and then they help them act on it.

Engaging employees around their personal purpose helps them connect more with their jobs. They find value in supporting the issues that are important to them, whether directly or indirectly. Helping employees contribute to a cause or effort engenders mutual respect and a sense of loyalty.

One way to start is by sponsoring employee workshops across the organization dedicated to finding meaning and purpose. Some of our clients have individuals design "story boards" of their own personal purpose. Imagine someone making a movie about what gives them purpose—identifying the elements that lend purpose to their lives and work. Think of story boards as like a movie about what matters to you. When engaged in their own self-discovery, employees connect more to the company purpose and the deeper meaning behind their jobs. Ideas often arise from these experiences that can move the organization forward. For example, strategies and action plans from such workshops can help teams focus the organization's efforts on common causes.

Too often we see companies trying to get their employees to connect to the company purpose without regard to their personal purpose. While well intentioned and necessary at some point, this is not the best place to start. To activate purpose, you need to start at the bottom, not the top, connecting people to their personal purpose and helping them discover what matters most to them.

John Mackey, co-CEO of Whole Foods Market, has learned this lesson firsthand. Mackey believes that while it is important to hire people committed to the company's values and purpose, to truly unlock their potential you need to redesign their work to make it more meaningful and assist them in discovering their intrinsic motivation for good. In an interview he said that "people want more than to just earn a living. They want meaning. They want purpose. They want to feel like their work is making a difference in the world."

In his book *Conscious Capitalism,* Mackey and coauthor Raj Sisodia go on to state that "to tap this deep wellspring of human motivation, companies need to shift from profit maximization to purpose maximization."[11] We understand that this shift can be difficult, as a delicate balancing act exists between purpose and profit.

EXERCISE *Activating Purpose in Others*

Personal values and meaning are greater motivators of people than organizational values. Discuss with your team members their values and what gives them a sense of purpose and meaning in life, both inside and outside the workplace.

Understanding your employees' values and purpose

- Outside of work, what are you passionate about in life? What do you love to do?

- What do you care about? What's important to you? What are your values, and what do you value most?

- What gives you a sense of purpose and meaning outside of work?

- How is your work meaningful to you? In what ways does your work make a difference?

Coaching and supporting your employees

- What can the organization do to help you connect your values to your work, both inside and outside the workplace?

- What difference would you like to make in the world? What work or opportunities inside or outside the organization could help you do that?

- What can the organization do to make the world a better place? What ideas do you have to help us do it?

Actively supporting employees' purpose as you do with their personal and career development plans

- Build purpose aspirations of team members, inside and outside the organization, into learning and development goals.

- Look for roles, jobs, and assignments that connect to your team members' values and purpose.

- Give employees the solution space to identify new opportunities for themselves and others.

- Recognize people when they reach a milestone or complete an assignment related to their purpose and meaning.

- Give employees opportunities to share or showcase purpose-related work with the team.

BEWARE OF THE TWO-HEADED PURPOSE MONSTER

This tension between the profit focus and the purpose focus can pose a challenge for leaders. Thomas Kolster, founder and creative director of the Goodvertising Agency in Denmark, is a leading adviser to companies on how to communicate purpose and sustainability. Kolster talks about this purpose/profit balancing act using the analogy of what he calls the "two-headed purpose monster."

If you think about purpose and profit as two heads talking, each in its own language and each moving in its own direction, you end up in a precarious situation. Kolster explains that this problem arises because companies have conflicting messages about purpose both internally and externally. He uses films and folklore to identify the common mistakes companies make regarding the dichotomy of purpose and profit. In doing so he identifies three types of two-headed monsters.

From Pixar's *Monsters University,* you might recall the characters Terri and Terry Perry, the two-headed monster. The Terri head is slightly smaller than the other, Terry, head. Now, which voice drowns out the other, purpose or profit? Which has the loudest voice in the organization? This monster is probably the most common one and is typical in organizations still struggling to implement purpose. For example, oil-and-gas companies tend to talk a lot about purpose and leading society toward a renewable future, but they consistently fall short of following through on the business model. Their profits outcry their purpose.

The second two-headed monster is the rather illusive though well-known Dr. Jekyll and Mr. Hyde. It does good in the light of day, but during the dark of the night pure profit rears its ugly head. The company weaves a great story, but it fails to pass the authenticity test for employees and customers. Volkswagen, for example, talked a good game about clean diesel all the while devising software to trick emissions tests.

The third monster is one worth watching out for: Superman. Think of Clark Kent as your average company. During regular business dealings, you wouldn't expect anything extraordinary from him, but when trouble arises he quickly turns into Superman, promising world salvation. It's an unexpected turn of events, which for most people can be difficult to believe.

Kolster says that he sees this superhero monster a lot in companies that jump on the purpose bandwagon, going from seemingly no purpose at all to speaking too loudly about one. The problem is that it feels forced and unclear. He also sees the Superman complex in companies that have a well-established purpose but that too often stay quiet about all the good they are doing—then they suddenly put a strong voice behind their actions. They need to *consistently* be modeling their purpose to employees, customers, and investors.

Kolster's advice when it comes to avoiding the two-headed purpose monster is to *KISS: keep it simple, stupid.* Think about these three monsters and which is most alive in your company:

- Loudest voice at the moment: profit and purpose compete

- Jekyll and Hyde: good in the daylight, evil after dark

- Superman complex: promising too much or staying too humble

What can you do personally to help resolve that two-headed monster at whatever level you lead? How can you help get clear on purpose and make sure it takes a front seat to profit when necessary?

DON'T BE AFRAID TO SHOW YOUR PASSION

When you get clear on your company's purpose and move it to the center of your organization, you will attract employees and customers who connect with you at that deeper relationship level. If you are not clear or you don't weave purpose throughout the organization—expressing the passion you have for that purpose—you're going to get a lukewarm commitment. If you have a magnetic clarity however—showing how your purpose is true, fits your business, and contributes to your success—people will buy in and follow you, whether customers or employees within your team or companywide.

Consider the outdoor clothing and sports gear company Patagonia. Its business is its cause, centered on "a love of wild and beautiful places." Fitting business with purpose, the company is committed to preserving natural habitats, slowing the decline of the environment, and advocating for the restoration, maintenance, and health of the planet. To leverage its environmental impact, the company donates at least 1 percent of its sales or 10 percent of its profits, whichever is greater, to grassroots environmental groups to support conservation efforts around the world.[12] When shopping at Patagonia, customers feel a sense of relationship with the company's history and cause. When they walk out of the store, they do so with more than clothing or gear: they walk out as participants in the Patagonia mission.

For those companies that are clear on their purpose, their customers' and employees' values, and their commitment to doing the right thing first, taking a stand—invoking a moral mandate—becomes a way of life.

As a self-described "activist company," Patagonia maintains an open leadership position on environmental causes. A visit to its website can begin with a call to support a current cause—"Defend Bears Ears National Monument," for example. In this case, the company provides a multimedia presentation to inform people about the issue and how they can get involved, leaving no doubt in anyone's mind what its mission is all about. The company is authentic. It stands for its principles, and it believes in and demonstrates them through action, putting skin in the game by providing time, resources, and energy to support the causes that it holds dear. Passion is key.

We are reminded of the time we met with a CEO of one of the largest companies in the world to talk about his company's efforts around purpose and sustainability. His company has been a leader in this regard, and we looked forward to the interview with anticipation. We fully expected a passionate, inspiring appeal for how business would play a role in making a future our children would want to live in. Instead we got a methodical litany of all the reasons why doing good made good business sense.

We were told that the millennials would demand it, that talent wanted it, and that social media was amplifying these "trends." He then went out of his way to tell us that "this is not some kind of moral crusade; it is simply good business." We know that doing good and having purpose is good business, but the fact that something is good *for* business is not necessarily inspiring. We decided to push him a little harder, hoping there was something more behind his company's decisions than the business case for purpose.

As the interview proceeded, we applied some pressure and asked more focused, in-depth questions. Finally, he said, "Well, look, we all can see that it's simply not working! We all want our children to be able to eat the same fish we can eat and enjoy the life we can enjoy." It had taken an hour-long interview, but the real passion behind the company's efforts had come to the fore. Suddenly, we felt inspired. His language changed as he talked further about sustainability and the company's conscious decisions that connected less with its financial goals and more with its purpose—its reason for doing business in the first place.

Getting started is difficult and activating purpose is tricky, but understanding the purpose that you want to embed in your organization will put you on the right track. Whether it begins with crafting a powerful purpose statement or answering questions on core values, activating purpose and advocating for your mission will unite your company around the revolution.

We talk more about the power of activating purpose in chapter 3, with a concept we simply call *branding from the inside out*. Purpose never works as merely an external marketing strategy, and in the end our leaders and employees are the ones who determine if the purpose has life.

BEST PRACTICES FOR
MOVING PURPOSE TO THE CENTER

- Know your company and articulate its place of true service, including why it exists in the first place and what it provides to customers, employees, and communities.

- If your company does not already have a purpose statement in addition to its mission statement, it's time to develop one. Better yet, if it's possible, write a purpose-driven mission statement stating both your direct goals and those that relate to your higher purpose as an organization.

- Conduct open dialogue with stakeholders inside and outside the organization, in person or online, to determine how the company is positioned to be an agent of good.

- Distill your company's higher purpose into well-defined programs with clear targets, metrics, and mechanisms for reporting back.

- Even if your company's products or services aren't directly contributing to a higher purpose, think of ways that you can still connect with one, even if it is more of an adjunct to your core business (like the Coca-Cola example).

- Figure out how to best fit purpose to your business by considering your customers, employees, and investors; their values; and their expectations about your company.

- Help employees activate their personal purpose by contributing to a cause or effort they care about. Translate this personal purpose into viable strategies and actions across the organization.

- Don't be afraid to claim a moral mandate and state loudly and clearly that you care about the present and future good of your customers, as well as society.

CHAPTER 3

Brand Purpose from
the Inside Out

I N 2016 OUR COMPANY, IZZO ASSOCIATES, SURVEYED 3,000 LEADERS at all levels in businesses that spanned a variety of sectors, asking them what concerns were discussed the most among their senior leadership. Of all the topics of focus on a leader's radar, we wanted to know which ones consistently topped the list. The number one answer we received from companies both small and large was "improving the image of our brand with customers." This response should come as little surprise given the highly competitive marketplace that most companies find themselves in today, but there is more than competition driving this relentless focus on brand reputation.

THE IMPORTANCE OF GOODWILL

One of the most important shifts in business over the past 30 years is the much larger share of company value attributable to goodwill. *Goodwill* is the established reputation of a business regarded as a quantifiable asset that represents the excess of the "fair market" value of the company's tangible assets (often referred to as *book value*). In other words, how consumers see our brand is often a larger portion of the company's value than its physical assets. Given the exponential growth of global consumers who now want to buy from socially responsible businesses, it's fair to say that a company's reputation is worth its weight in gold.

Uber: Scandal and the Loss of Goodwill

If you doubt that purpose and social responsibility matter when it comes to this critical but intangible asset called goodwill, think about the devastating impact of the numerous scandals Uber became embroiled in during 2017.

Since the tech-savvy ride-sharing and food delivery mobile app launched in 2011, Uber has been criticized for its labor practices, privacy issues, reports of sexual harassment of app users, and systemic problems within the company culture regarding diversity and sexism. In January 2017 a #DeleteUber campaign exploded when the company jacked up its rates in New York City around JFK Airport during a taxi protest over the White House's implementation of a widely controversial travel ban. The following month former Uber engineer Susan J. Fowler penned a blog post about the harassment and discrimination she experienced while at Uber, prompting other current and past female employees to come forward to share similar stories. And it didn't end there.[1]

In June 2017 board member David Bonderman resigned after making a sexist joke during an Uber staff meeting, which came on the heels of 20 Uber employees having been fired for a failure to address issues in regard to alleged sexism embedded in the company culture.[2] Shortly after, CEO Travis Kalanick was pressured out by Uber's largest investors, and executive Eric Alexander was fired after it was brought to light that he had obtained the medical records of a woman who was allegedly raped by an Uber driver and currently in the process of suing the company.[3]

Uber's goodwill was certainly not helped by the fact that during these 2017 scandals it was under federal investigation by the US Department of Justice, as well as a major lawsuit filed by Google parent company Alphabet Inc.'s self-driving car division, claiming that Uber had stolen autonomous vehicle technology. Even as of April 2017, these scandals were reported to have potentially decreased Uber's value by $10 billion.[4]

Time will tell if Uber can regain the trust of its customers, employees, and investors, but its near implosion in a fairly short time is astonishing. The once darling of Silicon Valley is experiencing firsthand what happens when social responsibility and purpose fall by the wayside. The lack of employee respect, specifically of female employees; an HR department that didn't properly handle reports of sexual harassment in the workplace; and unfair labor practices toward drivers—all led to a seemingly toxic culture. The Uber brand has taken a major hit, much of it resulting from this inability or unwillingness to support its workers. In turn, Uber's employees have spoken up and exposed the many issues that lie at the heart of this negative culture. On a recent Uber ride in San Francisco, a driver went so far as to ask us, "Do you know what it's like to work for a company you hate?!"

Today's organizations need to understand the power and importance of their employees and their relationship to the purpose revolution. Employees want to believe in what they're doing and work for companies that inspire positive change—not those appearing in the daily news under scandalous headlines. We believe that employees are *the* critical linchpin for thriving in the age of social good. When they talk, we need to listen, especially if they have an issue that needs to be addressed. And if we can instill mutual support and trust, they will become our biggest cheerleaders and an invaluable asset to the work that gets done, how it gets done, and how our goodwill is perceived by customers, and potential customers, throughout the world.

EMPLOYEES ARE YOUR BEST PURPOSE AMBASSADORS

For many businesses, especially larger ones, advertising, marketing, and social media are the primary ways that they try to harness goodwill.

In fact, most companies spend incredible amounts of money on efforts to convince consumers that theirs is a good and trustworthy brand. Given the cost, it may come as a surprise to most leaders that customers and potential customers are very skeptical about our communications about being good. Despite 58 percent of consumers agreeing that buying ethically produced products makes them feel good, there is skepticism about company ethics. Almost half (49 percent) say that companies often do good in one area but then hide the bad they are doing in other arenas.[5]

The same study found that "Half of Americans agree that marketing products as 'ethical' is just a way for companies to manipulate consumers."[6] The bottom line is that most consumers know that companies aren't going to tell us who they really are. After all, Volkswagen advertised its clean diesel technology for years, but the brand name is now synonymous with *emissions scandal*. Consumers assume that much of what we as companies tell them to be true likely isn't so.

But if customers don't much believe in advertising, whom *do* they trust? It turns out that they place much greater value in the word of employees than they do in public relations (PR) campaigns. When employees speak highly of a brand and what they say is consistent with the messages consumers receive about that brand, it is a powerful one-two punch. Findings from the 2014 Edelman Trust Barometer show that 52 percent of people trust what employees say about the company they work for over the company's official consumer communications. In other words, what your employees say about your company is more credible to outsiders than what the founder, CEO, or PR department reports to customers, shareholders, and the public.[7]

Our team members are the most consistent touch point that customers have with our brand, and if those team members believe in the goodness and purpose of our company, that message will reverberate with customers and potential customers in a powerful way. We have a name for this phenomenon: *branding from the inside out.*

BRANDING FROM THE INSIDE OUT

The idea of branding from the inside out is simple: every day our employees, both on the job and off, tell our story to customers and potential customers. If the people who work for you believe in your purpose and are enthusiastic advocates for the goodness of your brand, they will communicate this regularly. If they see that you're willing to put your money where your mouth is and actively strive to work toward your purpose, they will want to get out there and talk about the company's actions and positive attributes. They will take pride in their jobs and in telling people about the wonderful things your company is doing for them, for your customers, and for society. Your employees become more than just a group of workers clocking in and out—they became your brand ambassadors.

In our experience these brand ambassadors are much more believable than advertising or even the news media. Here is a simple example: John had flown more than 5 million miles on commercial carriers around the globe but had never flown with the low-cost Ireland-based Ryanair. He had read various articles about how Ryanair managed to cut costs to keep prices low and worried that if cheap seats were the airline's prime focus, attention to safety could potentially be lacking.

Before boarding one of its flights in Madrid, he met two Ryanair pilots and struck up a casual conversation, asking what it was like to work for the airline. The two pilots spoke enthusiastically about their experience. One of them volunteered, "Even though we focus on low cost, when it comes to maintenance and safety, we have a lot of faith in this company." Anything John had read in the media paled in comparison with a four-minute conversation with two real people who, without any probing, extolled the virtues of Ryanair's focus on keeping passengers safe.

Contrast that experience with a conversation John had years earlier after a fatal crash involving another airline. In 2000 Alaska

Airlines Flight 261 crashed off the coast of Southern California, killing all 88 passengers on board the MD-80 plane. It was soon discovered that poor maintenance and a culture that pushed mechanics to get planes out of the hangar were to blame. Only a few weeks after the crash, John was flying from Puerto Vallarta to Los Angeles with Alaska Airlines along the very same route and on the same type of plane.

During the flight he struck up a conversation with two flight attendants, who shared a memo with him that the CEO had just sent out, castigating whistle blowers for going outside the "family" to the media with their concerns about how maintenance was being conducted at the airline. Both flight attendants expressed deep disappointment in the CEO.

Given John's lifelong fascination with air travel, after the plane landed he asked the pilots how they felt. The pilots told him that they were now second-guessing every maintenance issue. They had lost faith in the airline's commitment to safety. You can bet John was grateful that he had arrived safely, and it was six years before he flew that carrier again. In fairness, Alaska Airlines has apparently regained a solid reputation both for safety and service, but imagine the damage caused by employees losing faith even for a short time in the company's most basic purpose: safe air travel.

The same brand ambassador phenomenon can be seen in the public sector. In the city where I—John—live, there is a central number that citizens can call if they have an issue of concern with municipal services—garbage pickup, water, street paving, parking tickets, and so on. I have called on numerous occasions, and the agents always seem deeply committed to solving my problem. On one occasion the agent spent 30 minutes helping solve a utility issue and kept saying, "No problem, it makes my day to help you out." Ironically, within two hours of that call my annual tax bill arrived in the mail. My first thought was something like *My taxes help fund salaries for people like that who really care about me and my city.*

Given that purpose is growing so quickly as a desired attribute for both talent and customers, it is critical that companies make great efforts to connect team members to their purpose. Team members must believe that those values are embodied in the company and in the everyday actions of its managers and other leaders. If they don't believe that, they won't just keep quiet; they may even become brand detractors, sharing their negative views and experiences with anyone who cares to listen. You risk losing talent, goodwill, and a positive brand image, one you've likely spent years fostering.

HOW TO MAKE EMPLOYEES AMBASSADORS FOR YOUR GOODWILL

Given that our employees have thousands of opportunities every day to communicate the purpose of our brand, and given that consumers are much more likely to believe them than our marketing efforts, it seems like companies ought to spend a great deal more effort helping team members believe in our purpose. Some companies work hard at this task; others not so much.

The folks at Hewlett-Packard told us that during all employee orientations, leaders and HR representatives emphasize the company's efforts around sustainability and social responsibility, linking it directly to the company's founding story. From the very start of an employee's tenure, HP wants team members to see a focus on the brand's purpose. The company expresses its goals, values, and objectives through something it calls "the HP Way." Built into these corporate objectives is a commitment to employees that states, "We demonstrate our commitment to employees by promoting and rewarding based on performance and *by creating a work environment that reflects our values* [italics added]."[8]

HP understands that the environment and culture that its employees are exposed to must connect directly to the values the company espouses, and it is willing to state this clearly and concisely. The company has a long history of leadership on issues such as philanthropy and environmental sustainability.

When we interviewed Don Guloien, former president and CEO of the financial services group Manulife Financial, he told us he believes that a critical part of his job is helping team members stay connected to the company's purpose: "To help people achieve their dreams and aspirations, by putting customers' needs first and providing the right advice and solutions."[9] Whether it's talking regularly about the way his company's products and services help people achieve those dreams or focusing on the importance of ethics in protecting people's assets, Guloien knows that team members are most engaged when they regularly see purpose as central to the business.

To ensure an ethical culture focused on doing the right thing, Manulife conducts team member surveys and asks employees whether they would feel supported if they raised an ethical issue that concerned them. The company wants to make sure that leaders have cultivated a climate in which people are comfortable advocating for doing the right thing. Guloien reiterates the company's commitment to customers and in so doing reinforces Manulife's goodwill and commitment to the values that its employees hold dear.

One way to think about this idea is that we constantly give our team members ammunition to be either brand ambassadors around purpose or brand detractors around shortcomings. If we fail them, our company fails too. It is imperative that we be responsive to employees' concerns and in tune with how they experience and understand our purpose. A company's brand is not simply the approval ratings of its product or service; it is inextricably tied to the people behind the brand, the ones who cause the company to do work that matters, to develop goodwill. One of the most important ways we ensure a work-force that brands us from the inside out positively and productively is by paying attention to what we call *moments of purpose congruence*.

Moments of Purpose Congruence: The Friendly Skies

Anyone familiar with customer service literature knows about moments of truth—interactions between a customer and a company that give the customer an opportunity to form an impression of the organization. These moments of truth can yield a customer for life or plant the seed for an all-out controversy. This makes the case of United Airlines particularly noteworthy.

For several decades the airline spent hundreds of millions of dollars building its brand around a simple tagline: *The Friendly Skies.* Then along came an incident, now infamous, on United Express Flight 3411. In April 2017 police dragged passenger David Dao from the overbooked flight after he refused to give up his seat as requested by the airline's management. In the process Dao incurred numerous injuries, including a concussion. Whether he had a legal right to stay on the plane may remain up for debate, but one thing is for sure: Dao is unlikely to fly with United again, and he will certainly not be singing the airline's praises anytime in the future.

As video of the passenger being forcibly removed went viral, and the media jumped all over the incident—especially after a relatively weak response from United's president and CEO Oscar Munoz—major issues in the carrier's operations were exposed and many consumers decided they wouldn't be flying with the airline in the near future.[10]

One could quip that United might need a new brand slogan: *The Friendly Skies, until we aren't—then we get really unfriendly.* Of course, these moments of purpose congruence that show our true colors can happen anytime, even in a purpose-driven company. How we handle such moments becomes the real test of purpose.

We believe that there are similar crucial points for team members—moments in which they become convinced that the organization either is serious about its purpose or is not. These moments of purpose congruence are decisive ones, and just like moments of truth—whether positive or negative—they often have a lasting impact. Consider the Alaska Airlines example earlier in the chapter. The accident and the resulting CEO memo that the flight attendants shared with John represent such a moment of purpose congruence, one in which the CEO failed.

An airline's most sacred duty or purpose is to get people safely from one place to another. Any failure to do so causes true dissonance.

Airline employees know that what they do matters—people's safety, their lives, and their families' lives are in the hands of the plane, its operators, and the company that owns it. The CEO memo admonishing employees seemed more concerned with the *appearance* of safety than the actual breaches that had occurred. It's a fair assumption that the CEO didn't intend that to be the message, but that was how it was received. The two flight attendants were visibly upset over the response. Rather than being positive ambassadors for the airline's commitment to the core purpose of safety, they had become brand detractors, or negative ambassadors. A moment of purpose congruence had failed, and it likely took quite some time before that moment was forgotten.

Walter Robb, co-CEO of Whole Foods Market, talked to us at length about how important it is that companies demonstrate that they are living their values in moments of purpose congruence. It is in these moments that employees make up their minds about whether the brand is truly purpose driven or if the values ring hollow. One such moment at Whole Foods is instructive.

One of Whole Foods' core values is environmental sustainability, as outlined in its mission statement under harnessing "human and material resources without devaluing the integrity of the individual or the planet's ecosystems."[11] In addition to providing healthy, organic foods, the company looks for ways to decrease its environmental footprint through such actions as building facilities using "sustainable material specifications combined with conscientious construction methods." In 1998 Whole Foods received the first Green Building Award for the renovation of its corporate headquarters, which showed a 42 percent construction waste reduction, and was profiled by the Environmental Protection Agency as a record setter in this area.[12]

In 2012 Whole Foods decided to further live its mission by discontinuing sales of any seafood that was not certified as sustainable. For some time the company had been labeling the appropriate seafood as "sustainable," but they continued to offer less-sustainable seafood products as well. It is one thing to provide customers with information about the sustainability of the products they purchase; it is quite another to turn away sales by deciding not to offer products your customers may want to buy because they are not aligned with your purpose.

Robb also talked about the goodwill Whole Foods received from team members when it made that decision: "People are looking to see if you really mean it, if your purpose is a living thing that you are willing to live when it might be easier not to." He also told us about how important it is that your values and purpose are a living document, one that expands and grows over time as the world changes around you. So even though solely providing sustainable seafood was not necessarily part of its original purpose, the increase of overfishing and the harmful effects it was having on the environment spurred the company to act. Whole Foods employees took notice.

Another example of an ideal moment of purpose congruence is a case with Synovus Financial, named the best company to work for in America by *Fortune* magazine in 1998. Shortly after the bank topped the list at *Fortune,* we made a visit to its headquarters in Columbus, Georgia, where we spent three days speaking to people within the company, gaining insight into its recent accolades. Nearly 20 years later, the lessons we learned still have an impact on us. John asked the then CEO of more than 30 years, James Blanchard, why he thought the bank was so successful. His simple response spoke volumes: "We love each other and we love our customers." Sounds a lot like purpose.

Blanchard went on to explain that one of the bank's core values was *Do the right thing.* Unlike typical corporate jargon regarding values, like the overuse of *integrity,* we loved the down-home clarity of this simple premise. After interviewing Blanchard, we had the opportunity to see this value put into practice. At the time, TSYS was a credit card processing company owned by Synovus, and a salesperson for the organization told us about a million-dollar contract he had turned down from a client. When we asked why, he said he felt that the client had the internal capacity to do the tasks themselves at a much lower cost. We were floored.

The salesperson turned down money that not only would have resulted in higher earnings for Synovus but would have likely boosted the salesperson's personal commission-based income as well. He told us, "It was the right thing to do, and the company had my back. They let me know that I had their support to do what was in the best interests of the client." He went on to explain that that experience made a big impact on his commitment to the bank. Synovus employees took the company's values seriously and were willing not only to respect it but to celebrate it. Even with the loss of a financial reward, everyone got on board to do the right thing.

Izzo Associates had our own moment of purpose congruence recently, when a large tobacco company reached out to us to help its leaders drive purpose within their workforce. The offer was lucrative, and there were myriad justifications we could have made for taking the business. The meeting planners we met seemed like good people, and we thought maybe we could make their day-to-day work lives better by improving the leaders' effectiveness. Perhaps we could even influence the company to be more purposeful and environmentally sustainable. Besides, it appeared to potentially be a large chunk of business.

What finally made the choice obvious for us, however, was imagining trying to explain the decision to work with a company in an industry that our core values just don't support. We knew that our employees of many years would disagree with the choice to work for a tobacco company, as we have always focused on working with socially responsible companies that add value to society. We could not imagine how we could justify our actions in choosing to work with such a company, but we could easily imagine the cynicism about our true values that it would engender among our own team. One team member said to us, "Phew, you had me nervous for a few days. If you had said yes, I'd have thought everything we stand for is a bunch of crap!" These are the kinds of considerations every leader at every level must have in every moment of purpose congruence that arises.

Examining moments of purpose congruence is an especially powerful way to separate companies that are genuine from those that are not. One millennial asked us, "How do you know if a company is just pretending to be purpose focused, just as some companies greenwash to look environmentally friendly?" She then answered her own question: "When I see that they have made a sacrifice for their purpose." She was referring to these very moments, when it becomes plain for all to see whether you really mean it.

What Happens When You Mess Up

Of course, we don't always do the right thing; as humans we all make mistakes, and hindsight is 20/20. We won't be perfect, and sometimes our products or services will inadvertently hurt our customers. How we respond to such breaches of purpose, however, are especially important moments that can show our best characters as organizations and individuals.

When we interviewed Don Guloien of Manulife, he told us about an investment product his company had offered to clients, one for which the company had failed to do its full due diligence, resulting in a loss of earnings. Instead of making excuses, Manulife honestly and publicly owned up to its mistake and made sure that affected clients got their money back. This was a crucial test of purpose congruence, and the company passed with high marks. Its response went a long way in sending the message internally, and externally, that purpose was for real.

Another example is how Samsung was lauded for how it handled the exploding Galaxy Note 7 smartphone in 2016. It was found that some customers' phones had batteries that would overheat, causing the device to literally catch fire. In response Samsung initially recalled 2.5 million phones but then widened the recall for *all* Galaxy Note 7s,[13] at an apparent cost of $2 billion.[14] The company put the interests of customers ahead of the short-term financial pain inflicted through recalls and replacements and in the process proved to employees why their goodwill is well deserved.

When breaches are not handled properly, employees will easily see through the charade. In fact, a large study by LRN, a leading provider of governance, ethics, and compliance management applications and services, found that more than one in three employed Americans has left a job because they disagreed with a company's business ethics.[15] The study found powerful links between a company's ability to foster an ethical corporate culture and an increased ability to attract, retain, and ensure productivity among US employees.

The results—based on telephone interviews conducted among a sample of full-time US workers as part of an omnibus survey by Opinion Research Corporation—showed that 94 percent of workers say it is "critical" or "important" that the company they work for is ethical. Currently, 56 percent of US workers define their current company as having an ethical culture. Yet one in four say that in the past six months they witnessed unethical, and even illegal, behavior where they work; among those only 11 percent say they were not affected by it.

If you are unable to prove to your employees why they should be brand ambassadors, there is no hope for the future of your organization in the purpose revolution. When was the last time your company did the right thing, even though it cost you a million dollars—or maybe many more millions in the short term? When did you stop offering products customers wanted because they were off-purpose? When did you fess up to a mistake instead of trying to cover it up with a PR campaign? Such moments of congruence are often the difference between closing the purpose gap and making it wider.

In closing the gap, your company creates goodwill and gives your employees something to believe in. When we make mistakes, we must come clean and move forward with the best intentions possible.

Do You Have an Internal Branding Campaign?

Most companies have external branding communication plans reinforced by traditional advertising and social media strategies. Companies often work hard crafting an image that moves external stakeholders toward supporting the brand—yet they don't always consider their employees' belief in the brand. The same intense effort must be made to communicate our purpose to our team members: if they don't truly believe it, our customers won't believe it, either. In fact, it is more important to sell your purpose *inside your company* than to promote your purpose to customers and potential customers.

Take WestJet, the Canadian airline, as a prime example. Providing true, caring service has been at the center of the brand from the start. The company's core slogan is *Owners care,* and at WestJet every employee is considered an owner. For many years the company has invested incredible effort in getting employees committed to its central purpose. It has conducted hundreds of sessions with employees to highlight, recognize, and praise the spirit of the slogan. When we worked with WestJet leaders, it seemed to us that they had spent more effort on internal branding than they had on external branding. The result was that their employees had become the best ambassadors for the caring brand.

There is a word of caution, however: Our internal purpose branding efforts must be less a form of promotion and more a commitment to demonstrate authenticity. When designing internal purpose branding campaigns, don't think of it as a marketing push but rather an authentic effort to connect people to your purpose. It begins at orientation when leaders talk about the true purpose of the company, as HP leaders do at every orientation. It is reinforced during regular daily meetings when reading the mission statement, at places like the Ritz-Carlton. It happens when leaders take the time to remind people what a difference we can make in the lives of our customers.

Auditing employee sentiment around the company's commitment to purpose will help uncover areas in which to improve. In some cases it's as simple as highlighting the actions taken toward supporting purpose—if your team members aren't kept informed about the important values-based decisions you're making, how will they know? Sending out weekly or monthly email updates that highlight how the company's recent actions relate to fulfilling your purpose informs employees about how your commitment to sustainability or other purpose-driven factors is being maintained. Larger companies should regularly send out key facts and stories about the company's fulfilling its purpose and ask leaders at all levels to spread those messages in meetings and daily interactions with team members.

Another way to brand internally is by encouraging employees to talk about or post information about the company and their experience through social media. You don't want to push too hard, but if you're doing the right thing, you will find that your employees *want* to act as your brand ambassadors. Most companies today, large and small, have some type of social media presence. Let your employees know that you want to hear their voices out there, too. Have your marketing team or HR department set up Facebook or LinkedIn groups for employees to express their thoughts, talk with one another, and share their stories with the outside world.

Every time we live our values and demonstrate that purpose comes first, we recruit brand ambassadors, and every time we fail to put purpose at the center, we convert our people to brand skeptics. If they believe in the work they do and know that their company isn't just giving lip service to purpose, they will help foster goodwill for the organization.

EXERCISE   *Time for a Purpose Audit?*

Most companies don't measure how connected their employees feel to their purpose, but we think every company should regularly perform what we call a *purpose audit.* A purpose audit asks employees whether they feel that the company is living its purpose and values and whether they see you "walk the talk." Even asking the question is an act of congruence. How you respond to the answers is even more important.

If someone audited your daily focus and communications to determine whether you enhanced or diminished team members' belief in your higher purpose, how would you rate?

Manulife Financial not only measures how team members perceive the company's ethics but also asks employees if they believe they would be supported if they reported unethical behavior up through the ranks. Former president and CEO Guloien told us, "Even by asking the question, you are sending a message. Then your culture becomes the best policeman you can have for living your purpose."

That purpose audit should ask questions such as these:

- Do you feel we are a purpose-focused company?
- Do you believe we live our values?
- If you see a breach of values, do you feel you would be supported for speaking up?
- Do you believe that our organization has the best interests of customers and society as our most important focus?
- Do you feel that our leaders focus on purpose more than profits?

THE CURIOUS CASE OF STEVE JOBS

Steve Jobs, the cofounder, chairman, and CEO of Apple Computer, is a singular case study of the ultimate brand ambassador. Though routinely believed to have been very difficult to work for and at times, well, a bit of a jerk in his own way, Jobs achieved iconic status that few leaders of his generation have. General Electric's Jack Welch may have been admired for his tenacity, but few people adore him in the way they do Jobs. Because of the work of the Bill & Melinda Gates Foundation, there is little doubt that one day there will be statues of Bill Gates in the developing world, commemorating him for fighting diseases like malaria. Still there has never been much of a cult around Gates. Jobs, however, stands among a chosen few business leaders who made a passionate connection to both employees and customers.

In the context of the purpose revolution, one might ask, "Why?" First, Jobs believed passionately in the products he created and their ability to transform lives. His mission statement for Apple Computer in 1980 was *To make a contribution to the world by making tools for the mind that advance humankind.*[16] He shaped both the Apple brand and the conversation around the brand both internally and externally.

For example, Apple is well known for its grandiose release of products in large gatherings. Jobs transformed those meetings into true events, hyping up the audience and ingratiating himself ever further to his employees and developers. With Jobs at the helm, Apple's purpose-driven mission yielded rare employee devotion and excitement that transferred over to customers.

On the surface the fierce loyalty of Apple users could appear to simply be about the products. Indeed most Mac and iPhone users wax emphatic about why Apple computers, smartphones, and tablets are superior to their competitors. Though the quality of technology can explain this oft-rabid loyalty in part, there is something more intangible that explains a deeper connection. When Jobs returned to the company after being fired by the board under John Scully, he said as much to the team at Apple.

The 1997 Think Different campaign that emerged after Jobs's return positioned Apple as a passionate advocate for "the crazy ones" who dare to think differently and change the world. The company associated its products with a set of values around disruptive innovation—to be an Apple user meant to be in the forefront of where humanity was heading. In interviews Jobs frequently spoke about the absolute necessity of "passion" and that the money never meant very much to him; it was always about the pursuit of something more. Product over profit or, put another way, purpose over profit! Jobs showed his employees that his true desire was to make the world a better place, and they followed him wholeheartedly.

At the end of the day, customers fell in love with Jobs's being in love with the brand, the technology, and his ability to create something new, authentic, and innovative. He cared about what he was doing, and he did it with a strong purpose in mind. The guy in the turtleneck was passionate about technology and how he felt it could change the world, and he spoke about it openly and honestly. The foolish bottom-line is that we loved Steve Jobs because we saw in him an incredible zeal for innovation and the role it played in human progress. When it comes to purpose, it can't be activated in a deep way if it is merely a means to an end; it needs to be about something larger, and we must boldly claim it and follow through.

EVERY LEADER IS A PURPOSE AMBASSADOR

It's easy to get duped into thinking that the only important moments of purpose congruence are the big ones, those that directly affect the course of a project, product, service, or company's overall goodwill. Of course, most of us as leaders and team members will not make these large systemwide decisions about the products we offer or be the ones in charge of making good on a broken promise for a faulty product. But day-to-day, moment to moment, it is the small ways we lead and operate that show who we are, what we believe, and how we support our purpose and mission.

For most team members, it is their experiences in their own work units that make them ambassadors for the brand. It has been said that all politics are local, and in some important aspect this is true of organizational purpose as well. Research has consistently shown that the frontline supervisor and the direct manager have a disproportionate impact on how a given team member sees the organization.[17] In this way the local team leader is the translator of the organization's purpose. The day-to-day moments often determine whether our employees think our purpose is real. Decisions about how we treat customers, whether we live the stated values, how individual leaders talk about our clients and our responsibility to society—it is in these moments that a culture is shaped.

No matter your position, you too have such moments of purpose congruence and you too are necessary to how customers and consumers understand the company, its purpose, and the overall brand. Without employee support, customers won't follow. And as we discuss in chapter 4, the customer must be your primary purpose.

BEST PRACTICES FOR
BUILDING PURPOSE FROM THE INSIDE OUT

- Emphasize your company's efforts around sustainability and social responsibility so that your employees see a direct link back to the company's founding story.

- Keep team members connected and engaged to the purpose of the company by regularly discussing how its products and services help people achieve their goals, desires, and dreams.

- In moments of purpose congruence, demonstrate to your employees and customers that the company and its leaders live the values they tout.

- When your company makes a mistake, don't hide from it: honestly and publicly own up to it and do whatever is in your power to make it right.

- Work on your internal branding efforts by highlighting, recognizing, and praising your company's purpose in employee meetings and internal communications.

- Perform a purpose audit of your daily focus and communication to determine whether you enhance team members' belief in your higher purpose or diminish it.

- Send out biweekly or monthly internal email updates to employees, highlighting how the company's recent actions fulfill its purpose. Use stories and key facts to make the updates tangible and relevant.

- Set up Facebook or LinkedIn groups for employees to express their thoughts, talk with one another, and share their stories with the outside world.

CHAPTER 4

Why Most Leaders and Companies Are Failing at Purpose

A GOOD FRIEND OF OURS, ALAN, HAS SPENT HIS ENTIRE CAREER working in the energy industry, mostly overseeing oil-drilling sites. We remember when he first signed on with a large company after years of working for smaller outfits. He was excited by their slogan, *beyond petroleum,* but even more impressed by the day-to-day way the company seemed to take safety and the environment seriously. The idea that an oil company could lead the effort toward a new energy future intrigued him. With pride Alan told us that for the first time in years he felt like he had found a company he truly wanted to work for. The company was British Petroleum, known to most everyone as simply BP, and it has since joined the ranks of companies whose names have become synonymous not for purpose and higher mission but for failing to put purpose at the center of the business. Alan left BP a year after the oil spill in the Gulf of Mexico, his initial optimism unfortunately long gone.

This well-known example represents the tip of a much more important iceberg. As the Ernst & Young/Harvard study clearly shows, most senior leaders and business owners see the value of being purpose driven and most likely have a set of personal values leaning toward the decent-human-being side of the equation.[1] Yet in our experience, most businesses, small and large, are losing at purpose—or at the very least are failing to achieve the high levels of engagement and competitive advantage available in the age of social good.

Our experience over the past 25 years is that most leaders spend an inordinate amount of time focused on the numbers and beating their competition, without truly embracing the balancing force of purpose. It's not that the heads of these corporations don't care—well, some don't—but the majority want to do right by their employees and customers and provide value, or at least do no harm, to society and the planet. These leaders and business owners *want* to do good, but it's hard!

It's easy to get bogged down in the bottom line, especially if you're running a large company that reports to stockholders and other investors. If you run a smaller company, just staying alive and winning enough business can naturally make us concentrate more on finances than contributions. At times leaders and managers are focused on simply getting through the workweek like many of their employees. The problem, of course, is that in a time of major transition, this laissez-faire attitude no longer cuts it. The purpose revolution is here, and if you're not taking part, you're losing out.

Still, even companies and leaders who recognize this fact have a hard time getting on board with purpose. They may not have the right mind-set or the necessary resources at their disposable. Maybe they think they understand what it means to "have purpose" and therefore try to fake it until they make it. But no matter how hard you try, you can't fake purpose. In working and speaking with hundreds of company leaders, HR representatives, and employees at all levels, we have unearthed some of the reasons why companies fail to truly close the purpose gap or activate purpose. Dissecting these key reasons gives insight on how to avoid missteps or dead ends and pursue purpose in earnest.

PURPOSE IS NOT A STRATEGY

Purpose isn't a strategy, yet many leaders make the mistake of treating purpose just like any other plan to win talent and customers. They believe that if they approach pursuing purpose in an organization mostly as a means rather than an end in and of itself, they're in the clear. They ask, "Isn't it OK to simply focus on the fact that employees and customers want us to have purpose and therefore we ought to pursue it like we would every other business strategy?" At face value this seems like a reasonable question. There is nothing wrong with a powerful dual focus on the business and values-based case for purpose. In fact, almost all the leaders and companies we interviewed who are succeeding at driving purpose are very clear that doing good is good business. There is no contradiction per se between purpose as a good for itself and purpose as means to greater loyalty among stakeholders. But there is a catch, and it turns out to be a large one, in answering this question.

The fact is that people see through the focus on purpose solely for the sake of business. We have worked with more than 500 companies around the world, and it is obvious to us that employees can detect the difference between purpose that is genuine and purpose that is purely about business. The same is true for individual leaders. Our people can tell when we care mostly about the numbers, even if we don't intend to communicate that. This mind-set does us a disservice and shows disrespect for the people who support us. Humanist and physician Albert Schweitzer is purported to have once said, "I've never seen a good definition of *soul,* but I always know it when I see it." We believe that a similar idea applies to today's purpose-driven leaders: there's something that's hard to define, but it's possible to tell when they're serious about practicing what they preach.

There is also a very practical side to why purpose as a means won't work over the long term. Sooner or later a choice will be required between the short- or even medium-term interests of the business and your higher purpose. Only when leaders are truly connected to that purpose can those short-term traps be avoided. Normally, we find that bad decisions that expose a false sense of purpose are made in line with short-term business strategies, not long-term sustainability goals. Take the aforementioned Volkswagen emissions scandal. The decision to deceive regulators on emissions from diesel cars was clearly good for business in the short term, as it allowed the company to promote and sell its vehicles as "clean alternatives." But what allowed that decision to be made?

Our best guess is that VW was not staffed by evil people who could care less about the environment. Instead there is a very good chance that the focus on clean vehicles at VW was being driven mostly as a strategy rather than as a belief in doing what's right and making the world a better place. The distinction between "doing what's right" and the business case may feel like mere semantics, and there is no doubt that the difference can be subtle. There are the occasional companies like Enron, run by people whose basic ethics turn out to be purely self-oriented, but most of the biggest purpose problems likely come from this focus on purpose as a means rather than an end.

You must truly connect to a deeper quest and find ways to communicate it to the organization and your customers. It is also necessary not just to explain the commitment you're making but to show how you're pursuing that purpose. Make sure that members of your organization at all levels understand that this pursuit is not a passing trend but rather a major change in how business is being conducted today—and will continue to be conducted in the future. Just as in investing, a focus on the long term keeps you grounded and away from knee-jerk reactions to fluctuations in the industry or market, and it leads to higher performance over time.

MONEY IS NOT A PURPOSE

As was stated earlier, for organizations we define *purpose* as an aspirational reason for being that is about making life better now and in the future for all stakeholders, especially customers, society, and the planet. In reading that definition, please note that the words *money, profit, revenue,* or even *shareholders* or *investments* are nowhere to be found. A purpose is at the heart of what we do as people to make the world better and to feel proud of our jobs, decisions, and overall lives. Making money is not a purpose.

This is not to say that a purpose-driven company cannot or should not be focused on making money or generating incredible profits. On the contrary, as mentioned, research shows that companies that activate purpose are even more profitable than those that have less sense of purpose. The point is whether profit or purpose is the main driver. As Dolf van den Brink, CEO of Heineken Mexico featured in chapter 1, made clear, "Most people don't have a personal purpose just to make money." Yet as leaders we often forget this at our peril because a consistent focus on the bottom line rarely activates deep commitment.

Ironically, almost all companies' original genesis was to solve a problem. In this way most successful companies begin with a sense of purpose, and that very purpose to solve a real problem for a group of people was the engine of their early growth. Great companies began by focusing on their product or service rather than on making a profit. Steve Jobs was famous for having preached this idea as necessary to success. The greatest challenge over time, however, is that as companies grow, their products become so diverse and the pressure to produce economies of scale becomes so strong that the intent to serve becomes subservient to the need to produce profits. The two are deeply related, but over time the goal of generating growth, even if it does not serve customers or the greater society, takes over.

From our experience, whenever making money becomes a company's primary purpose, losing sight of what's best for customers and the world at large, it is often the beginning of a downward spiral that can be halted only when purpose once again becomes paramount. This is a dance, of course, because profits do matter, but sustainable profits are almost always an outgrowth of serving a purpose.

Take Dell Technologies, for example. Founded by Michael Dell in 1984, the company grew massively in its first 20 years. When he left the company in 2004, however, it fell on hard times. Fast-forward three years, and in 2007 Dell returned to refocus the company on its core purpose, going so far as to take the company private in an effort to make it the "largest start-up in history."[2] Since that time the company's performance has improved, with increased customer satisfaction and its highest employee satisfaction scores ever.[3] The company has continued to grow, with one of the largest technology company acquisitions in history in 2015.

One thing we always tell leaders is that most people who work for you don't care how much money the company makes. They probably don't even care about how fast it grows or the increase in sales year over year, even though these factors are routinely the primary focus of a senior leader's communications. Employees do care about being on a winning team; they want the company to make enough money that their jobs are secure, and they enjoy the intellectual puzzle of figuring out how to provide even better products and services. But what drives most employees more than anything is the pride they feel in having done a good job, of producing something that they know meets a real need. While there are, and always will be, team members primarily motivated by financial reward, this is not where the trend is headed. Employees need deeper satisfaction in line with their personal values and goals, and your company needs to help them achieve this going forward. As hockey great Wayne Gretzky said, you gotta skate to where the puck is going.

EXERCISE   *Money versus Purpose*

Imagine that a group of people came into your office as objective observers to listen in on the daily communication in your team or company.

- How easy would it be for them to identify the problem you're trying to solve and the purpose that you support?

- Would they mostly hear about profit-and-loss statements or growth targets?

- Would purpose be mentioned at all?

- As they see which employee actions are reprimanded and which are rewarded, both financially and informally, what would they say seems to be at the core of your leadership or organizational culture?

Write down the answers to these questions and then ask, *Is purpose or money at the center of my team and this company?*

If you feel that the scale is tipping toward money over purpose, it's time to reframe the approach. Call a meeting with your team or other colleagues to discuss the company's purpose, beginning with the problem you're all tasked with solving. Provide examples of how your company has met the needs of consumers in the past and why it's important to maintain this commitment today. Open the discussion so that you can hear from others about their motivations at work and how they see purpose playing out—or not—every day.

These types of meetings can be difficult, as they ask people to open up about feelings around purpose, something that isn't always highly supported in the corporate world. You must therefore go into the meeting prepared, willing to share your own feelings; point to concrete examples within your company or others that exhibit the strength of having a purpose deeper than "making money" (and please feel free to use those we present throughout the book!).

Often starting a dialogue to build a deeper connection to a true purpose is all it takes to activate purpose and close the purpose gap.

Here are some questions to pose to open a dialogue:

- If purpose were the main focus of our business or team, how would our meetings be different?

- What questions would we ask as leaders on a more regular basis?

- What would we highlight, recognize, and reward differently?

PURPOSE IS NOT A MARKETING PROGRAM

The third reason companies fail to truly activate purpose is because they treat it as though it were a marketing program. Using purpose as a marketing effort will not ingratiate your company or cause with employees, customers, or investors. Like viewing purpose as a means, if you don't believe in it and support it, it won't pass muster.

Carol Cone, CEO of Carol Cone on Purpose, told us that to thrive in the purpose world, companies will "need to align their core competency as a brand with their social platform; they will need to make a clear purpose statement." She adds that "they will need to measure and share their impact and be honest about their warts."

The centrality of being authentic, open, and honest with customers is echoed by Steven Althaus, global director of brand management and marketing services at BMW, who said, "Marketing will no longer be the department that puts lipstick on the gorilla. It needs to be about truth well told."[4]

One of the best ways to get a quick take on whether purpose and social good are at the heart of an enterprise, and not just a way to push products or services, is to see who is "in charge" of it. Though we have the utmost respect for people who do the marketing function in companies, it is always a concern to us when social responsibility, sustainability, or purpose are housed in the marketing or communications department. Ideally, purpose is owned by every leader and every team member in the organization, embedded in the very way they do business.

Leaders at companies like 3M and Ford who are working hard to foster purpose-driven cultures emphasized how important it is to embed purpose into every job, especially on the operational side of the business. Senior leaders in particular must be careful not to outsource purpose. As Muhtar Kent told us, "The CEO or business owner should also be the chief sustainability officer."

The reason is simple: if you want to truly activate purpose, it is best to have marketing amplify a purpose that already exists rather than promote one as a strategy. There is nothing wrong with expressing your purpose loudly and clearly, exposing consumers and communities to your mission and values, but purpose must first be realized and embraced from the inside. If your marketing team professes a vision that is not in line with the company's reality, cynicism will be bred among the ranks of employees, and customers will be able to sniff out your disingenuousness. What's more, it sets up the potential for a game-changing disconnect between the "marketing purpose" and the "lived purpose."

LIVED PURPOSE VERSUS MARKETING PURPOSE

A *lived purpose* is one that a company's leaders and team members rally around and support through every action, every day. When you live your purpose at work, you take your company's mission statement seriously and hold yourself, and your coworkers, up to the highest standards related to your stated purpose. The companies that have a lived purpose are leading the charge in the purpose revolution.

The *marketing purpose,* however, only describes the stated purpose to the public, whether or not the organization and its members have truly embraced it.

It is more important to have purpose and live it authentically than it is to simply tell people you have purpose. When you *live* purpose, you show it—it guides your strategy, your decision making, your allocation of resources, and your relationships with customers, your community, and one another. People recognize and appreciate these efforts. When you market purpose, you're only telling people about it, not showing them. Just because a company comes up with a catchy slogan to tell people that it's in on the trend doesn't mean it's taking the necessary action to stay in step with what's going on in the world.

We have seen this focus on the marketing purpose backfire many times. One such organization had slick, well-produced videos that told the story of the company's purpose both to employees and customers. But there turned out to be a lot more sizzle than steak, and though customers may not have seen through it, employees often talked to us about the reality behind the story communicated in the videos. As one team member said bluntly, "We all make fun of the videos because we see every day that profits, not purpose, are the focus of this company."

A company like Procter & Gamble (P&G) meets the high standards that it sets in its purpose-centered mission: *touching and improving lives.* As a multinational manufacturer of a wide range of products—including cleaning products, household items, and personal care and hygiene—P&G is constantly in public view and needs to ensure that its commitments to environmental sustainability and social responsibility come across authentically and are supported by its actions.

P&G's brand director for northern Europe, Roisin Donnelly, understands this idea firsthand: "Marketers' campaigns can be seen by millions of people. Your brands are a positive force for good—both for people and profit. But changing the world starts with your purpose."[5] Over the years P&G's marketing efforts have been fully in line with its purpose, as seen in such campaigns as 2014's "Like a Girl," by its feminine hygiene brand Always.

The ads featured boys, young men, and young women who were told to perform actions "like a girl," such as running or throwing a ball. Their responses were to feign weakness, act overdramatically, and put on airs of timidity and restraint. When preadolescent girls were asked to do the same actions "like a girl," they performed them with strength, agility, and vigor. The ad then asks the question *When did doing something "like a girl" become negative?* and ties it to how these negative stereotypes can do real harm to girls as they mature into women.

Donnelly stated that before people saw the ad, only 19 percent considered "like a girl" to be a positive statement; after the ad it jumped to 76 percent. According to Donnelly, the ad "has built trust that girls and women have in themselves and could make a huge difference to the planet in the future."[6]

But even at companies like P&G, leaders must constantly ensure that the stated purpose fits with the day-to-day experience of employees and customers. For every company that has a slogan or campaign that it lives up to, there are just as many that start with a marketing plan but are unable to do the hard work to make their purpose a reality. We see this idea play out every day, especially due to the rapid change that business and society are experiencing. Your marketing plan must be up with the times, but it also needs to be authentic to your company's purpose.

LEADERS MAKE PURPOSE A ONE-WAY STREET

Another reason why organizations often fail to close the purpose gap between employee and customer purpose-driven expectations and the company's reality is that purpose is led as a top-down effort with little genuine involvement from team members or customers. Many leaders think that the way to activate purpose is to give people a purpose. They discuss ideas with other executives or senior managers and then write up a set of values that they think make sense. They articulate a lofty vision alongside a compelling mission and then push the idea out through HR and internal marketing channels, trying to sell that purpose to team members.

There is an inherent problem with this top-down approach. It turns out that employees are motivated and engaged primarily by their *own* values—not the company's. Research shows that when employees are clear on their own values and feel that they can live them at work, they are far more engaged, even regardless of the company's values.[7] It is not that the company's principles and purpose don't matter; they do. The problem is we forget that ultimately people activate purpose when they find it for themselves.

For example, when Darren Entwistle became the CEO of TELUS, a large Canadian telecommunications company, he knew there was a need for a new set of values that could take the company forward into a highly competitive and rapidly changing landscape. Just as 66 percent of executives are profoundly rethinking their purpose due to the current disruptive environment,[8] Entwistle knew that he had to get serious and focus on purpose—but not just any purpose. Rather than have executives determine the values, he commissioned an exercise to tap into the values of thousands of TELUS team members. The values that emerged—such as *courage to innovate* and *spirited teamwork*— grew directly out of what employees said mattered to them most. These values became the backbone of the company's transformation, which we discuss in chapter 7.

This early work building the values from the bottom up laid a firm foundation for the emergence of a strong culture at TELUS that was embraced by associates. The senior team might well have come up with similar values, but taking the time to engage thousands of team members was a worthy investment.

In our experience leaders often forget that the *conversation* about purpose, mission, and values is just as important as the well-crafted statements that result from such an exercise. Town Shoes Limited (TSL), a Canadian division of DSW Inc., went through a similar process while crafting its purpose statement. President Simon Nankervis engaged leaders at all levels to identify the *why* behind the brand. He included a broad group of team members in the process, and the word *happiness* turned out to be incredibly sticky. The purpose that emerged—*happiness through self-expression*—felt like something everyone could get excited about.

Encouraging people to identify their own core values and how they can be expressed at work helps activate purpose in individuals. The core principle to remember is that purpose comes from the inside more than from the outside. Leaders who truly close the purpose gap know that the focus cannot be simply to give people a purpose; they must help people find their *own* purpose and live it through their work every day. As leaders, whether we lead a small team or a large multinational, our job is to help people see the connection between their values and the organization's work.

PURPOSE IS STUCK ON THE WALL

Years ago John was consulting with a large company that had a grand purpose and set of values posted prominently on the wall of every office, framed behind a nice pane of glass. One day a middle manager at the company casually told John, "That is exactly where the values are in this company—on the wall and under the glass but never alive in the room." Unfortunately, we see this situation all the time: companies failing because their purpose is stuck to the wall.

Many companies mistake idealistic statements for purpose. Such declarations are nice—and useful in many cases—but unless they are, as Walter Robb of Whole Foods told us, "a living document, alive in the daily work and decisions," they won't activate much purpose in your organization.

A principle to keep in mind here is that *the conversation about purpose is more important than the articulation.* A well-articulated purpose is good, but what determines its effectiveness in a company is how alive the conversation about that purpose is. As an example, we have done a great deal of work with hotels and hotel chains around the world. Almost every hotel has a lofty statement of purpose emblazoned somewhere in the staff room, extolling the virtues of serving customers, but those statements mostly hang on the wall, collecting dust. The hotels that truly activate purpose do so because their leaders are constantly asking how they can make the purpose more than just a statement, how it can become a living, breathing document.

Wayne Shusko, former general manager of the Park Hotel in Charlotte, North Carolina, used to make the purpose of *truly serving guests* come to life by attending every employee orientation and telling stories of team members exceeding guests' highest expectations, thus fulfilling the purpose of service. In these meetings Shusko connected with his employees, scraping the statement off the wall and helping them understand its deeper meaning. He recognized people based on that mission and made a big deal of it, highlighting their related accomplishments. Though it seems like a simple gesture, it is so rarely done.

Leaders need to find systemic ways to keep purpose "off the wall" and in the work. That may mean reading the mission statement at every meeting or making sure that every big decision is vetted with purpose in mind. You, your team, and your organization must examine how this purpose statement plays out every day. If it's not easy to detect, it's likely stuck on the wall, where it will do no good and provide little to no impact.

WHEN YOUR PURPOSE IS NOT RELEVANT

There is one final reason why companies often fail to powerfully activate purpose: sometimes your purpose doesn't keep up with the times.

For purpose to truly stay relevant, it must not only remain constant but also capture changes in the context in which your business or team thrives.

Walmart, for example, has always centered its purpose around value and low prices. When John was invited to the company's headquarters in Arkansas to speak to hundreds of leaders in its healthcare division, he witnessed firsthand the almost religious zeal among leaders in the pharmacies over what was known as the $5 prescription. It was an effort to reduce the price of the drugs most commonly used by US seniors to $5 or less per month.

At the same time, Walmart leaders told John about the focus within the company on what was called "the next-generation Walmart customer." The idea was simple: Walmart had become the largest company in the world by winning the previous-generation customer, who seemed to care about low prices over everything else. Today the company is well aware that the next-generation Walmart customer (and team member) has more on their mind. Younger customers still want low prices, but as is typical of the other members of the purpose revolution, they also want to consume in a way that causes less harm to the planet.

Sustainability and the environment were not part of the purpose equation at Walmart for many years. One could even argue that the focus on low prices at any cost potentially drove more environmental degradation. In recent years Walmart's low-prices purpose has been joined by a purpose to make a greener planet. The company still has work to do on wages and benefits, but any objective analysis would show that it has become a major force for devising a more sustainable supply chain while reducing its own environmental footprint. This is a great example of a company that evolved its purpose in accordance with a changing set of concerns among stakeholders.

Every company should ask periodically whether its purpose must evolve to changing needs in society. It's important to regularly take stock of your mission to ensure that it still fits in a contemporary context.

For example, Facebook, launched in 2004, has grown immensely over time. What was once a way for college students to connect with friends online has turned into a social media behemoth with 2 billion users, revolutionizing the way people interact.

For more than a decade, Facebook had proclaimed that its mission was *to give people the power to share and make the world more open and connected.* It's a strong statement, but in the face of changing realities it seems to fall somewhat flat. Today we are seeing steady disillusionment with the role that business plays in society. From the financial collapse of 2008 to accelerating global problems such as climate change and income inequality, citizens around the globe both blame business for these problems and increasingly look to business to solve them.

Facebook cofounder, chairman, and CEO Mark Zuckerberg recognized this reality and how it affects his company's customers. Whereas connecting users was once enough, Zuckerberg believes that Facebook's mission can go much deeper. "You also need to do this work of building common ground so that way we can all move forward together," he said.[9]

In June 2017 Facebook unveiled its new mission: *To give people the power to build community and bring the world closer together.* The company is providing new tools to help users build better Facebook groups and engender a greater sense of community. It is also taking steps to fit this purpose into the company's practices, for example by providing to Facebook group administrators more open data about when users are most active.

Even a company like Facebook, which seems far from failing, is moving forward when it comes to purpose. Zuckerberg knows that the mission is important and must truly connect with Facebook's employees and customers. The previous fit wasn't quite right, so they took the next step, ensuring success for many years to come.

BEST PRACTICES FOR
AVOIDING PURPOSE PITFALLS

- Your purpose must be authentic and cannot be viewed as another short-term business strategy or way to garner customer attention. Emphasizing a long-term view will help keep your purpose present in any major decisions your company makes.

- Shift the dialogue from profit to purpose. Dedicate time in meetings to discuss why purpose is more important than profits in the changing business landscape. Get people on board with your ideas and help them connect to the initial problem the company aimed to tackle when it first began.

- Align your brand's core competencies with your social platform by making a clear, authentic purpose statement.

- Make sure that purpose, sustainability, and social responsibility are not housed solely in the marketing or communications office but are instead owned by every leader and team member in the organization. Everyone should own purpose—not just the marketing team.

- If you want to truly activate purpose, have marketing amplify a purpose that already exists rather than promote one as a strategy.

- Ask yourself and your team how to make purpose more than just a statement but a living, breathing document.

- Recognize team members when they contribute directly to your company's purpose and highlight their related accomplishments.

- Be willing to update your purpose and vision with the changing times, keeping in mind the expectations of tomorrow's generation as well as today's.

Leading a Purpose-Driven Culture

Now that you understand the contours and benefits of the purpose revolution, as well as how to define company purpose and avoid the traps along the way, it's time to dig in and get practical. The large study by Harvard referenced in part one showed that while leaders believed that purpose would make a significant positive difference for their businesses, more than half felt they were doing a poor job of activating purpose and embedding it in their culture.

In part two we show you how to lead in a way that brings purpose to life for your company and team. Whether you are a CEO, senior executive, business owner, or frontline leader, you will learn practical skills for leading with purpose. We show you the importance of having and communicating your personal purpose, as well as how to drive job purpose and not just job function. You will discover how to get your employees and customers truly engaged in your purpose in a hands-on way, how to create a line of sight so that every team member feels connected to purpose, and how to make your team or company a talent magnet through purpose. The final chapter summarizes eight key practices for purpose-driven leaders.

CHAPTER 5

Every Leader Must Have a Purpose

J OHN REPLOGLE IS THE CHAIRMAN OF THE SOCIAL MISSION BOARD and the former CEO of Seventh Generation, one of the companies leading the purpose revolution. When Replogle was 35 years old, he was president of Guinness Bass Import Company and managing director of Guinness Great Britain. He was a successful executive who felt like he had "life on a string." His work and life had meaning for him, and it didn't particularly feel like anything was missing. While serving in that role, he began working with a mentor, who encouraged him to write a personal mission statement. He wasn't getting much traction on it until one day when he was rushing off in the car with his young children in the backseat; he was thinking about that assignment when he glimpsed his children's eyes in the rearview mirror.

"I looked at them and realized that everything I had done in my career to that point was for *me*, and I felt I hadn't done anything to make the world they would live in a better place." He said he started to cry as he realized that making money was simply not enough. Months later he left Guinness to take a job at Unilever and eventually the CEO position at Seventh Generation. "I knew a change was needed," he told us. "I wanted my work to serve a higher aim." In that moment this leader discovered his true purpose. To lead a purpose-driven culture, everything starts with us as leaders asking the kinds of questions Replogle asked himself that day.

There is growing consensus among leaders today that business exists to make the world better, and most agree that both employees and customers want to associate with enterprises that provide a sense of purpose. Ninety percent of executives have said that their company understands the importance of purpose, but "only 46 percent said it informs their strategic and operational decision-making."[1] We see two reasons that explain this disparity.

First, as discussed, leaders at all levels—managers, executives, and business owners—have simply never been taught to lead for purpose. And this makes sense given the prevailing business paradigm. Leaders rarely have exposure to formal or informal instruction about business being an agency for good in society, nor have they been helped to see the powerful way that purpose drives employee performance and business success. We lack sound models, tools, and methods to own and drive purpose in our organizations. Additionally, most of us as leaders have had few, if any, mentors or role models to inspire purpose-centered leadership.

Second, most leaders have been schooled in the philosophy that business exists primarily to make profit and increase shareholder value. Sure, we provide jobs, make great products, and offer services that help people, but at the end of the day we're here to make money. This is how the health and vitality of our company is measured, and over the past century this has been the prevailing mind-set. This is not to say that leaders and business owners are backing away from their responsibilities to society; it's just that they need help in understanding how to lead with purpose and why it's so important.

Leading in the purpose revolution must begin with each of us as a leader discovering our own purpose—the reason we are leading that is greater than the massing of profits. You need to find your personal purpose to contribute to something that is greater than yourself or even your company. Your actions must be imbued with meaning because what you say and do matters, maybe even more than you realize. It's not just a question of your values but of your future and legacy, and it all starts with finding and living your purpose.

MAKE YOUR PURPOSE PERSONAL

In chapter 2 we introduced the idea that you can embed purpose in your organization by helping employees activate their own personal purpose at work. This idea applies across all levels of a company but maybe most importantly to leaders. It has been our experience that you can't lead purpose or activate purpose in others if you don't have purpose yourself. As Henri Nouwen wrote in his book *The Wounded Healer,* "The great illusion of leadership is to think that man can be led out of the desert by someone who has never been there."[2] Closing the purpose gap must begin with leaders authentically connecting with their own purpose. You can't lead others where you have not been.

Leadership purpose is rooted in your values and your authentic self. You must be true to who you really are and to the ethics, principles, and causes that are most meaningful to you. From this place, you will be able to establish a clear mission in life, focus attention on what is most important, find courage to do what is right, and, as a leader, activate purpose in others. In considering your personal purpose, you need to be honest about your deepest values and know how to leverage your unique, distinctive qualities, skills, and position to make a difference, to your people, your customers, and the world.

A great example of a leader who found his personal purpose—transforming the company he worked for in the process—is Paul Polman, CEO of the consumer goods company Unilever. He calls on leaders to use their position to take a stand and be courageous about what they believe in. When Polman joined Unilever, he helped refocus the business around social and environmental values. Under his leadership Unilever created the Sustainable Living Plan, which includes plans to "reduce our absolute environmental impact...and increase our positive social impact."[3] He realized that addressing these issues required a fearless long-term strategy, not short-term thinking. He told *Forbes:*

> The big changes we need to make to transform this world, if you want to, are changes that will be made against the odds—lots of naysayers and skeptics.

> So to fundamentally make these changes, you need to have a certain level of courage, especially at the CEO level...[so] we certainly need more courageous leaders.

Defining *courage* as "the ability to put the interests of others ahead of your own and be able to absorb personal risks," he encourages us "to fight your way through that."[4] Having met scores of Unilever team members at all levels, we can personally attest to the way Polman's personal purpose, and his willingness to speak openly about it, has inspired deep loyalty and commitment throughout the company.

Subhanu Saxena, managing director and global CEO of the pharmaceutical company Cipla, based in India, takes the reflection of his personal purpose even deeper, showing the importance of connecting people's work to a sense of meaning and purpose beyond themselves: "People come to work feeling they are doing Mahatma Gandhi's work and that has been embodied by our senior leadership team. It gives passion and dedication to the organization and I really see that come out in our people."[5]

SAP, a leading global software company based in Germany, has a long history of civic engagement. The company's stated purpose is *to help the world run better and improve people's lives.* SAP CEO William R. McDermott has engaged personally with global leaders and heads of state to advocate for achieving the United Nations Sustainable Development Goals, using his personal capital to demonstrate commitment to these global aims. Recognition for these efforts came when the RadleyYeldar Fit for Purpose Index of the top 100 most purposeful brands in the world was announced in 2016. SAP's #20 ranking positioned it as the top technology company in the index, ahead of HP, Microsoft, Intel, Cisco, Google, IBM, and Facebook.[6]

It is just this courageous willingness to share personal purpose that will be required in the purpose revolution. As leaders, at our peril we forget that people are waiting for us to inspire them. They want to hear and see our personal purpose, whether we own the business, are the CEO, or lead a team.

WHAT IS YOUR PURPOSE?

In Frank Capra's 1946 film *It's a Wonderful Life*, George Bailey is given the opportunity to see what the world would be like if he'd never existed. A frustrated businessman at the end of his rope, Bailey attempts suicide only to be rescued by his guardian angel. The angel shows Bailey what the world would have been like had he never been born and in so doing demonstrates to Bailey his contribution to the world—how he enriched the lives of his family, friends, and community.

Consider for a moment what the world (your team, your family, your community, your colleagues) would be missing without you. What causes might be left out? What work would not be started or would be left unfinished? Imagine all the people in your life—at home, at work, in your community—who are better off because of your presence. How come? What do you provide, and what can you offer going forward, as a leader who will make a difference? Developing personal purpose involves getting in touch with our values and our unique contribution to the world.

As you think about your own purpose as a leader, you need to clarify your deepest values and concentrate on what sincerely matters to you. To help uncover your purpose, we recommend writing a personal purpose statement based on your responses to a series of introspective questions. Developing your purpose statement will keep you focused at work and throughout your career on those things that are most important to you.

It is becoming more common to see leaders writing their own purpose statements in the context of the purpose revolution.

At Unilever, for example, all leaders at the VP level and above attend a weeklong session where they craft a personal mission. This kind of exercise should be done in every organization, small and large, with leaders being encouraged to take time to ask, *What is my purpose?*

In our interviews we asked numerous leaders to share their purpose statements. It was obvious that they had thought about these statements carefully and developed them fully. One of our favorites came from Dolf van den Brink, CEO of Heineken Mexico: *To be the gardener, with boundless curious energy, to grow a better world.*

Here are some others we have collected or read over the years:

Denise M. Morrison, president and CEO of Campbell Soup Company: *To serve as a leader, live a balanced life and apply ethical principles to make a significant difference.*

Amanda Steinberg, founder of Dailyworth.com: *To use my gifts of intelligence, charisma, and serial optimism to cultivate the self-worth and net worth of women around the world.*

Sanjeev Saxena, CEO of POC Medical Systems: *To develop next-generation diagnostics to provide a better life.*

All of these statements look inward but are implemented through outward actions. These executives describe their aspirations to become better leaders, lead better lives, serve others around the world, and rally for the causes that are important to them as individuals.

The whole point of devising such a statement is to help you focus on your purpose. Think about how this purpose relates to your position or situation in life, your leadership role, and your ability to influence others and make a positive difference. If you're the CEO, for example, you have a major opportunity to weave your purpose into the fabric of the company culture—its attitudes and methods—and move it forward. But leaders at all levels, no matter the size of their business, can benefit from articulating a simple purpose that is communicated clearly. We all feel more connected to leaders who have a purpose and can articulate it, whether it's the CEO or our immediate supervisor.

EXERCISE   *Write Your Own Personal Purpose Statement*

There are four foundational purpose elements that we touch on in this chapter that you need to consider when writing your purpose statement:

- Leadership purpose is personal, emerging from your heart; it is rooted in your values—your authentic self. It leverages your unique and distinctive qualities, skills, and position. Key questions to ask yourself are *Who am I—my unique life experiences, values, and qualities? What drives me? When do I feel most engaged?*

- Purpose is transcendent. It ties you to what matters most, to something bigger than yourself, something enduring that offers a deeper sense of meaning. Purpose connects your place as a leader to the larger world of relationships and events.

- Purpose is altruistic. It is not about you but about the well-being of people and environment outside yourself—how you enrich society or the planet.

- Purpose is forward thinking. It points you and others forward toward a compelling vision, focusing attention and energy on the creation of a better future reality.

Take Amanda Steinberg's purpose statement, for example: *To use my gifts of intelligence, charisma, and serial optimism to cultivate the self-worth and net worth of women around the world.* She hits on all four elements in a concise, authentic way. Her gifts of intelligence, charisma, and optimism are personal; her commitment to cultivating the worth of women around the world is both transcendent and altruistic; and the statement is compelling and forward thinking in focusing on the ongoing struggle women experience every day, even in contemporary society in developed nations.

Start with reflection. Take a look at the following questions and jot down quick responses.

- *Who am I? What are my unique life experiences, skills, values and qualities?*

- *What drives me? When do I feel most engaged?*

- *What do I believe in? How do I connect my life and work to something bigger than myself?*

- *What makes my life worthwhile, meaningful, and fulfilling?*

- *What are the core sources of my meaning and purpose?*

- *What is my reason for being?*

- *How do I want to make the world better? For whom? Where? How?*

From your reflections, write down your answers to the following questions.

Personal

- What have you always been excited about? What did you always love to do even as a child? Tell a story about this or give an example or two.

- Describe one of the most meaningful experiences or times in your life. How has this influenced who you are today?

- What are you passionate about now? What gets you up in the morning?

Transcendent and Altruistic

- What do you connect to or embrace to guide your life? What higher spiritual, moral, or humanistic ethic guides your life? This is something enduring, bigger than yourself.

- What causes do you believe in? What difference would you like to make in the world to better society or the planet?

Now craft your personal purpose statement.

- What themes and patterns emerged about yourself from your reflective work?

- What matters most to you? What gives your life purpose and meaning? When do you feel most engaged?

▪ What makes your life valuable, worthwhile, and fulfilling? What is your reason for being?

Make a list of the words and phrases that come to mind. Don't worry about a statement at first—just note your impressions. Once you have a list of words that resonate with you, craft them into your personal purpose statement—a simple sentence or two is all you need!

Also consider the noble or higher purpose that's at work for you now. How does your purpose influence or shape how you lead?

THE LEGACY QUESTION

One of the most powerful ways we have discovered to unleash a leader's personal purpose is to have them consider what we call the *legacy question:* What do you want your legacy to be after you leave this company or team?

Research by Morela Hernandez and her colleagues suggests that the idea of "legacy" is a stronger driver of "stewardship behavior" than even altruism.[7] In fact, they found that introducing the idea of death and mortality helped people think about what they will leave behind for others. By *stewardship behavior* we mean a focus on the impact that your work has on others, especially those who follow, such as the younger generation. Connecting people to their personal legacy and what they will be remembered for is quite powerful.

In our extensive work coaching leaders and business owners, we have discovered that asking the question *What do you want your legacy to be?* elicits very different answers than do questions like *What do you want your goals to be?* Time and again we have seen how the conversation in a room changes when you ask leaders this simple question—*legacy* is a powerful word. Rarely do their responses focus on profits, revenue, or market share. Instead they tend to talk about the difference they have made in the lives of employees, customers, the community, and their industry. When they connect to their legacy, they become aware of their higher and perhaps truest aspirations.

A few years ago, John did a series of speaking events for the Mayo Clinic in a room on its main campus in Rochester, Minnesota, called the Founders' Auditorium. The large room has black-and-white photographs on the wall, including a large one of the Mayo brothers, as well as pictures from early days at St. Mary's Hospital, long before the clinic's now worldwide reputation dating from the 1920s on. John said, "Being in this room, it is not hard to realize that each of us is part of a story that began long before we came into this room. We will only be in this room for a short period of time, and one day we will only be a picture on the side of the wall—or maybe a fading memory of someone who once sat here in living color. The only question worth pondering is whether the room will be better in the future because you were once here."

Afterward many leaders said that that was the most impactful part of the two-hour session for them. Immediately, they began to connect to their true sense of purpose, asking, *Why am I here, and what will be the legacy of my having been here?*

If you work with leaders as a consultant or coach and want to get them thinking about purpose, we strongly suggest shifting your conversation to focus on legacy. Start by emphasizing legacy in a client's personal life. Many leaders have been trained so vehemently to think of legacy in terms of traditional business results that it may be difficult at first to get them to think about what they really want to be known for in the future.

John remembers vividly the first time he asked Darren Entwistle of TELUS that question. The response was "In every generation there are only a few legacy companies that are remembered for having been true exemplars in business. I want this company to be one of those few." As John did a series of speaking events across the company to more than 15,000 TELUS team members, he shared the simple personal legacy voiced by the CEO. The response was overwhelmingly positive. TELUS employees at all levels found the idea compelling. They wanted to help leave a legacy as one of those few companies in each generation that mattered.

EXERCISE *Identify Your Legacy*

As a leader it is imperative to identify the legacy you want to leave behind. Take some time to answer the following five questions.

- How will the world be better because of your presence and your contributions?

- How will your family be better in the future because of your actions?

- How will those who work for you be better in the future (or even their children's future) because you were their leader?

- How might the lives of your customers and community be better because of the actions you take as a leader, at whatever level you might be?

- What are four or five words or phrases you would want people to use to describe your influence on them or the world?

Keep in mind that you're considering these questions regarding not only your professional life but more importantly your personal life. Some may be hard to answer, but doing so honestly will guide your actions and help you lead others through any situation with your purpose intact.

PURPOSEFUL LEADERSHIP MATTERS—*A LOT!*

All the truly purpose-driven organizations we worked with and researched have a founder, CEO, or other executive leading the charge. This is true at Coca-Cola, 3M, TELUS, Unilever, Cipla, Ford, Heineken Mexico, Seventh Generation, and Whole Foods. They all have a clear sense of their mission and purpose and work hard to bring it to life through the organization. We firmly believe that the purpose of the CEO or business owner matters a lot when building a purpose-centered organization.

The CEO's Purpose

We found that a CEO or business owner acting as a champion of purpose makes a huge difference in any organization aspiring to its higher purpose. They are better positioned than anyone else in the company to put higher purpose on the road map. To make it a strategic priority, they can shape a vision that includes purpose and frame higher-purpose outcomes as key indicators of organizational health. In our discussion Muhtar Kent of Coca-Cola said, "The CEO has to be a champion and a visionary of sustainability. Sometimes sustainability requires a big investment and oftentimes balances risks and rewards. You have to be willing to see that, steward it, and value it."

CEOs are also in a unique position of leverage, as their decisions and mandates can have a huge impact on realizing the company's higher purpose, not just internally but externally and down the supply chain. For example, Bill Ford, executive chairman of Ford Motor Company, told us, "One thing CEOs can do, which is what we've done, is to really push our supply base, to demand things of our supply base in terms of product—recyclable, sustainable products that go into cars and trucks. We are also demanding things like human rights behaviors from our supply base, not just the tier ones but as far down as we can see. This has certainly changed behavior because if you want to do business with us, you need to do the following things."

Leading from their personal purpose, CEOs inspire the executive team and others in the organization to find their own purpose and to drive for higher purpose in the organization. Kent told us that he "found inspiration from my own leaders, such as Robert Woodruff, who led Coca-Cola for more than half of the twentieth century. He was committed to making a positive difference in our home city of Atlanta and beyond."

Leading with purpose in this way leaves a lasting impact on the next generation as well. Kent said that "in many ways we are still following in Robert's footsteps when it comes to sustainability and building stronger communities." We see the same effect at Cipla, where generations of leaders at the top level consistently focused on higher purpose, deepening the organization's sustained commitment to that purpose over time, no matter the business, industry, or market conditions.

Leaders direct attention, which in turn gives permission for things to happen downline in the organization. In this way CEOs—by championing purpose and modeling the way—legitimize the various activities and the use of time and resources directed toward reaching the targets of higher purpose. There is a powerful principle of human behavior underlying the influence of attention on individual and group behavior—the fact that what we pay attention to grows, partly because, as Otto Scharmer, author of *Theory U*, tells us, "energy follows attention."[8] All that being said, just because you're not the CEO doesn't mean you can't pursue your purpose and mission to its fullest extent.

Every Leader Is Someone's CEO

As important as the CEO is, for most people in the organization their direct supervisor might as well be the CEO. No matter your title—executive, manager, director, supervisor, associate—if you are leading others, you are the person with whom your team members have the greatest contact and connection. You are the one whose actions, priorities, and values most influence their day-to-day work experience. And to them you are the face of the enterprise.

Although a company, even a very large one, appears from the outside to be a single entity, it is a set of interconnected teams. Each of those teams has a leader, and each part of the organization has its own measure of how to drive purpose and to what extent. We have seen many individual leaders in large enterprises who deeply connect to their own purpose and in so doing are beacons of purpose in the larger entity.

This is the case at Qantas Airways, an Australian company we have been privileged to advise over several years. Qantas is often named as one of the safest airlines in the world, if not *the* safest. We have witnessed the way an unrelenting focus on safety at all levels unifies and brings purpose to the company. Maybe even more importantly, we've seen the direct impact of Qantas's leaders, at all levels, talking about what the company meant to them personally as it navigated a financial crisis. The engine of motivation was activated as the question became a personal one: *Why does it matter to me that this company survives and thrives?* This is a critical question for any leader to answer.

Leaders spoke eloquently about how Qantas represented the Australian spirit to the entire world. We personally watched the positive reaction of frontline team members to this transparent view into the inner purpose of leaders and could tell how deeply it moved them. And it wasn't just the CEO who spurred that motivation—it was the individual leaders authentically talking about the true purpose of the airline and their own work. When we as leaders find our purpose, we infuse that spirit and energy into the rest of the organization. A stronger connection is made as we encourage our team members, employees, and colleagues to find their own purpose and discover how it aligns with the company's mission.

Both of us, Jeff and John, experienced early in our own careers the impact of a direct leader when we worked for a woman named Trudy Sopp, who ran a department of the City of San Diego. Sopp was head of the organization effectiveness team. She consistently reminded us that our work with the city's various departments could make a big difference in the lives of employees and citizens. It was also clear that she had a personal purpose to help each of us reach our fullest potential. This purpose was contagious, and we watched as that sense of mission influenced even leaders above her, including the city manager, John Lockwood. Trudy not only managed one of the most highly engaged departments in the entire 12,000-person municipal workforce but she inspired many of us to go through our own careers deeply connected to purpose. She may not have had the title of CEO, but to us that's exactly what she was.

When it comes to purpose, we often forget how important we are to those we lead, no matter our official title or level in the organization. Don't be shy about sharing your personal purpose or focus with those above you. Remember, whatever your title, you are someone's CEO. Name your purpose and share it boldly.

BILL FORD AND A BETTER WORLD

Bill Ford, executive chairman of Ford Motor Company and the great-grandson of Henry Ford, is a near singular example of what it means to lead with an unclouded sense of personal values and purpose. Sitting face-to-face with Ford at his headquarters office in Dearborn, it is immediately obvious that purpose is important to him. His clear blue eyes show a steady resolve about what he wants to accomplish in the world. He has always loved the outdoors and as a young man would "spend every minute I could in the woods of northern Michigan." While attending Princeton University, Ford was exposed to new ideas about the impact of industry on the environment. He read Rachel Carson and Edward Abbey, and their words resonated with him profoundly.

Returning to Michigan after college to work in the family business, Ford would again visit the north woods, but things were changing. He noticed "a lot of environmental degradation happened up there over the years, and when I came back after graduation I was absolutely appalled by the lack of recognition [at Ford Motor] that these issues existed. And it bothered me—to the point that I thought, *I don't know if I can stay here at this company.*" Ford decided to stay but only under one condition. He made a commitment to himself: "*I will stay if I can change it.* It was a fairly naive thing for a 22-year-old, but at the time it was important to me, so I just plunged ahead."

Ford felt the tension between what he saw and what he wanted. He resolved to stay with the company not because he saw a clear path but because he imagined that with the right effort he could forge one. Leading from his deeper values gave him the sense of personal purpose and mission, enabling him to drive sustainability practices at Ford Motor.

He realized that his family name allowed him to take a stronger stand on environmental issues within the company than other employees could. Knowing how to use his position for good was imperative to his personal purpose. But even then, he said,

> I was kind of written off in many circles in the company as somewhat of a nut case. Early on I was criticized for being a leader on environmental issues. It was no fun because going back to the '90s and early 2000s when I started speaking out about this, there was literally no support anywhere, neither in the business world and certainly not in the industrial world. Even the NGOs [nongovernmental organizations] disliked me, perhaps as much as the business world because they assumed I must be a wolf in sheep's clothing.

Even though Ford felt like he was on the fringe for standing up for the environment, he stayed in the game. Why? Because he was in a position to do something about what he believed in, and it was a cause worth fighting for. He stood by his values and acted with courage, bringing his purpose to life and influencing his every move in the company. He loved the outdoors; a clean environment was important to him, and he knew it was to others. He understood that there was a way to build cars and make a profit without sacrificing his values along the way.

He told us, "I believe—and I've always believed—that a company should exist only if it's actually making people's lives better; if not, then it probably shouldn't exist, so that meant the same in our case. I felt we had to remove any barriers to that, and the environmental impact was becoming a big barrier." For Ford that was bigger than the environment and extended to improving the lives of Ford Motors' employees, customers, and community—and not just for today but for the next generation.

"In my case," he said, "I'm working for my children and my grandchildren because I hope that they are going to be part of the leadership of this company someday, and therefore I care about the company they are inheriting and what legacy they are inheriting." He went on to say, "You act differently when your name is on the side of the building and will be there long after you are gone."

Of course, every leader's name will be remembered by their team; whether it is remembered in a positive or negative light depends on the leader's purpose, mission, and actions. Leaders must consider what they'll be remembered for. In Ford's case, we're willing to go out on a limb and say his legacy of sustainability is likely to take hold and last for generations. Having met with Ford and some of the team members charged with sustainability at Ford Motors, it is imminently clear that those who run the company see this purpose—what was once only Bill Ford's purpose—as part of its long-term mission and lasting legacy.

BEST PRACTICES FOR
LEADING WITH PURPOSE

- To lead with purpose, you must be true to the principles, ethics, and causes that are most meaningful to you and leverage your unique, distinctive qualities, skills, and position to bring them to life.

- Take the advice of Paul Polman of Unilever and put the interests of others ahead of your own and absorb the risks and the attacks you will receive from naysayers.

- Develop a fearless long-term strategy, not short-term thinking, when it comes to personal purpose and leading your team.

- Direct your primary focus toward enriching others or some cause or purpose outside yourself, combining the transcendent with the personal.

- Instead of always asking yourself what *goals* you want to achieve, reframe the question and ask, *What do I want my legacy to be?*

- Talk to leaders you admire, both within and outside your organization, about their potentially acting as your "purpose mentor."

- Write a personal purpose statement based on the four foundational purpose elements discussed in this chapter. Refer to this statement regularly, especially when making tough decisions and discussing potential new programs and initiatives.

- As a leader, focus on your higher purpose to deepen the organization's sustained commitment over time. Your direct attention matters, and it grants permission for things to happen downline in the organization.

CHAPTER 6

Drive Job Purpose, Not Job Function

THE SPANISH WORD FOR "JOB," *TRABAJO*, IS A DERIVATIVE OF THE Vulgar Latin word for "torture."[1] Of course, most people don't see their jobs as a form of cruel punishment, but the truth is that most jobs are simply too small for the human beings inhabiting them. The purpose gap for employees results from their desire to find meaning and purpose in their jobs, beyond financial reward, but realizing that their jobs are often mostly just a means to an end. When we connect to the true purpose of our work, however, it is transformed from a means to an end to an end in and of itself. How people see, understand, and experience their jobs and work has a profound impact on their commitment and performance.

THE PARADOX OF ZOOKEEPERS

Take the curious case of zookeepers. Although eight of 10 zookeepers have university degrees, their average annual salary is quite low compared with what these professionals might find in other settings, such as private-sector scientific research or teaching at a university. The typical zookeeper job description involves scrubbing enclosures, scooping waste, and spending time outside in the elements, and there's often little room for career advancement. This is exactly why university researchers Stuart Bunderson and Jeffery Thompson have studied work satisfaction and commitment among these workers.[2]

In spite of the aforementioned drawbacks, the researchers found that most zookeepers are deeply satisfied with their work and even have a sense that they were "born to do this job"; they also have a strong sense of purpose about what zoos accomplish. To us the reason behind this satisfaction is simple: For the zookeepers, the job is not just a job; it has true meaning to them. It is an important part of their identity, a calling they have answered.

In the survey of senior executives conducted by Harvard University in collaboration with Ernst & Young, one of the real gaps that emerged between the desire to activate purpose and reality was the skill of leaders to make purpose come to life in their organizations and unleash its energy. One of the biggest reasons why companies fail at purpose is that they assume their leaders know how to drive purpose in their teams.[3] The truth is that most leaders have never had training on how to lead for purpose. Organizations train leaders in how to communicate, how to hold people accountable, how to organize meetings, how to be more engaging leaders, and how to do better forecasting; but when it comes to leading for purpose, we simply assume that they know how to do it. Well, they don't!

It's not that leaders don't believe in the power of purpose. In fact, according to a June 2017 report by the EY Beacon Institute, 73 percent of business leaders say that corporate purpose is a key to success in navigating the uncertainties of the economy and today's volatile world.[4] Instilling a sense of purpose and acting on it, however, requires that leaders know how to communicate job *purpose*, not simply job *function*. As leaders we need to learn to articulate the company's mission and how it relates to the purpose of each individual on our team.

To truly accelerate performance and win over the emerging workforce in the purpose revolution, leaders must consistently work hard to help all employees see their work not just as a career but as a calling. The task is not so much to change the work people do as it is to help them reframe their mind-set around their job. Employees must be able to find and understand the intrinsic purpose in their work. Whether you're a CEO, small-business owner, midlevel manager, or

HR representative, you can be integral in ushering along this process, helping employees find meaning while also increasing their performance. In the process, you are facilitating the development of a culture of purpose. Let's start looking at this process by exploring the concept of a calling as compared with a job or career.

HOW PEOPLE SEE THEIR JOBS MATTERS—*A LOT!*

For almost two decades, Dr. Amy Wrzesniewski, an associate professor of organizational behavior at Yale University's School of Management, has been studying how people view their work. Her research has revealed that most people see their work in one of three ways.[5] Some see their work as simply a job, something they do for the related external benefits they receive. These people trade their time for something else, typically money or security. Their work neither is a stepping-stone to some other career or learning experience nor holds a source of deep meaning to them. She calls this approach to work a *job orientation.*

Wrzesniewski refers to a second way that people see their work as a *career orientation.* In this case the job is a source of learning and growth, as well as a stepping-stone to the next career move the person hopes to make. Work is not merely a way to make a living but an important building block in a long-term, successful career. Each position the person holds is a step often taken with a planned career trajectory in sight. The focus is on climbing the ladder and achieving greater work status.

The third way is known as a *calling orientation,* in which people see their job not as means to an end but an end itself. This idea comes from the Latin word *vocatio,* which was used to describe a religious vocation. In Wrzesniewski's research, the idea of a calling is about seeing a way in which your work provides a true service, as well as something that you feel is core to your identity. You find purpose and meaning in what you do, and you feel a type of reverence for the work you perform and its importance to the world.

Research by Wrzesniewski, and others who have used her framework, has clearly demonstrated that when people see their job as a calling, they are more engaged, satisfied, and committed to the organization. They also are less inclined to leave their employer, and even call in sick less often than those who perceive their work as a job or a career.[6]

While the research shows that many factors influence our overall thoughts and feelings about our jobs, including how our parents saw their jobs, it also suggests that the specific type of work we do is not a strong predictor of them. For example, there are surgeons who see their work as simply a job, and there are hotel housekeepers who consider their work a calling. There are also individuals doing the very same job who see it in different ways: while one person considers it "just a job," another may see it as a career, and a third as a calling.

This idea mirrors something we discovered in 1994 while conducting research for the book *Awakening Corporate Soul.*[7] We interviewed 3,000 people, asking them to identify times in their careers when they felt most engaged and believed they had performed at their highest level. Not surprisingly, two of the most important elements in their responses were whether they felt they were contributing to something meaningful in their job, in terms of service, and whether the job was a good fit for their talents. Research has shown that if we feel we are serving an important purpose and the job matches our capabilities, we are more likely to see our work as a calling. Leaders play a major role in influencing both of these factors. Let's first look at helping others discover purpose, and then we'll discuss job fit and its relationship to purpose.

JOB PURPOSE VERSUS JOB FUNCTION

One of the most important concepts for purpose-driven leaders to understand is the distinction between job function and job purpose. *Job function* is the set of tasks a person performs in their role, whereas *job purpose* is the intended outcome of the job in terms of its impact on customers or society. For example, consider a person who is responsible for issuing building permits in a municipality. Their job function is to process the permits, but their job purpose might be to ensure public safety by requiring contractors and homeowners to meet specific standards. Their purpose could also be helping contractors and homeowners perform work that is necessary to their livelihoods and that improves their lives.

Even particular tasks within a larger role can be reimagined and focused on purpose. For example, having worked with hundreds of companies, we know that conducting performance reviews is not the favorite part of most managers' jobs. The reason for this can often be found in a focus on function rather than purpose. The function of performance reviews is to rate employees and serve as a basis for promotion and pay decisions. But the higher purpose holds so much more. Performance reviews provide feedback that improves a person's career or life. They help ensure that customers and clients receive the best possible service. These reviews also contribute to the company's ultimate success, providing job security for those who work there.

The Walt Disney Company has always been a proponent of differentiating between function and purpose. In Disney amusement parks, they like to say that no matter your job function, your job purpose is spreading happiness. Though the function might be to collect tickets, clean bathrooms, perform in a show, or clerk in a gift shop, the purpose of every person's job is to make the park guests happier. It's not hard to imagine how this mind-set helps bring more purpose to jobs that might otherwise seem less meaningful.

When you can help people connect with their job purpose—so that they see it as separate from their job function—they discover how their position can be a calling and not merely a job. Their engagement and performance will increase, and they will be more content at work and in their personal lives. Explaining purpose to others and driving purpose in an organization take practice, but once mastered these skills can make a big difference to the success of a team or company.

HELPING PEOPLE FIND PURPOSE

Leading a culture of purpose begins by helping people imagine the higher purpose of the tasks that they do on a regular basis. This requires us to speak of work in larger terms, and it takes courage to talk about job purpose over function. Some people are embarrassed to discuss this aspect of work, or they think that it's better to keep their distance and maintain a detached or apathetic attitude. Others fear that rallying around purpose might come across as insincere or disingenuous, as if they are trying to manipulate their team members. Our advice is to stop worrying and start inspiring. If you're serious and sincere, others will recognize your good intentions, and you'll be able to begin driving purpose throughout your organization.

John has a personal example of the simple ways you can drive job purpose through honesty and open conversation. When his second book, *Values Shift: Recruiting, Retaining and Engaging the Multi-generational Workforce,* was published, it was still in the days when direct mail had a big impact on book sales. The team members in his consulting business were sending personalized mailers to directors of human resources to promote bulk sales of the book. When John, out on a weeklong road trip giving talks, checked in with the team by phone on Tuesday morning, they seemed discouraged. "Well, in case you forgot," a team member lamented, "we are stuffing envelopes all this week, and it's not much fun."

John said he understood that it wasn't the most rewarding task but that he hoped they would remember how his previous book helped change many people's companies, jobs, and lives. He went on to say, "I don't really know how many people will open those envelopes. I don't know how many books we will sell. But somewhere in those letters we send this week, you are going to change someone's life. We aren't stuffing envelopes [job function], we are changing lives [job purpose]." Having given his most inspirational advice, he was discouraged when the team member casually responded, "Well, thanks. Do you have anything else? Because we are kind of busy."

For the rest of the week, John didn't bother to ask about the envelope stuffing when he called his team to check in. When he returned to the office on Friday afternoon, though, he noticed a small but profound change there. On the wall where the team was tracking sales of the book, the metric of "books sold" had been replaced by "lives changed." He said: "Okay, guys, I know you put that up for me."

The team corrected him. One team member said,

> Well, actually, when you got off the phone with Susan, we made fun of you: "Easy for him to say that we are changing lives; he's not stuffing envelopes."

> But halfway through the next day, Alison joked as she stuffed an envelope, "This is the one—changing a life here."

> By Wednesday we started talking about it. We realized we don't sell books just to make money; we do it because we really care about the lives of the people we're trying to help. The task was still a bit unpleasant, but suddenly it had meaning.

This simple story illustrates the subtle way that leaders can help people shift their thinking about the functions of their job toward its purpose.

To drive purpose and connect employees with their job purpose over their job function, directly explain the greater value behind their tasks. For example, consider someone who works as a service representative on the floor of a large hardware store like Home Depot. They might have the job function of answering customers' questions and stocking the shelves, but their purpose might be to help customers find cost-effective solutions to their problems and to empower them to learn new skills. It may be necessary to reiterate this point during one-on-one or group meetings, but once employees internalize it, they're likely to view their jobs in a different, more positive way. When employees understand that they are contributing to a larger overall effort, they feel a sense of connection to their work, their colleagues, and the organization's purpose.

Note that this idea applies to teams as well. Just as every role and person needs to define purpose, so too must entire teams. When teams work together to define and articulate the purpose of their work, they tend to maintain focus and feel more positive about the job they're performing together. When teams begin to seriously entertain the question of team purpose and not just team function, the conversations move people toward higher engagement. Every team should have a purpose and not just a function, and every team should help shape the way they see their purpose.

REMINDING PEOPLE OF THE DIFFERENCE THEY MAKE

Our client Molly Maid is one of the leading home-cleaning services in the world. When we agreed to do a full-day workshop on leading for purpose and engagement with the franchise owners, we asked (as we often do before such events) for the names of some of the more successful franchisees to interview ahead of the session. In speaking with them, we found that their success was due, in significant part, to discovering and driving purpose over task.

One of the most successful franchise owners was a young woman who, though relatively new to the business, was doing particularly well. As she discussed leading her team, she told us that "cleaning other people's homes is sometimes tough business and can be very repetitive." She said that from the first moment she hires someone, and then frequently in her weekly team meetings and one-on-one discussions, she tells her people to never forget that they are giving their clients "the most important gift you can give another human being." What is that gift? Time.

"I tell them that time is the most precious gift a human being has and that their work is giving that gift to our clients. With time freed up from cleaning their homes, they can spend more time with their kids, more time on their hobbies, and more time on the things that are most important to them in their life. We aren't just cleaning homes; we are giving people the gift of time!" She constantly reminds her people that they are doing noble work that is serving others. It was no surprise to us that her franchise was outperforming on customer service, profits, and staff retention.

Molly Maid also had us speak with the owner of the largest franchise in Canada. He attributes his success as much to higher purpose as to a thorough cleaning of a house or an apartment. During our discussion he talked about the fact that many of his clients are older people who may not get many visitors. He therefore encourages his employees to take a few extra minutes to chat with clients when they arrive on-site or before they leave. He challenges his team to reframe their work toward a higher purpose: helping alleviate loneliness. Both the employees and the clients appreciate these conversations, which result in stronger relationships, loyal customers, and happier employees.

Another example relates to members of the financial services industry. We were working with a large retail bank that was trying to get its customer service representatives to upsell clients on more of the bank's services. From a business perspective, the function of this is to "get a larger share of wallet." In other words, the bank wants its customers to bring as many of their financial needs and products— loans, credit cards, investment accounts, and the like—to the bank as possible, rather than use another company's services. While there is nothing untoward about wanting a larger share of the business a customer might have available, we discovered that when leaders focused on the purpose behind this upselling, rather than merely the function, sales increased.

The leaders who helped service representatives see the way these products and services could help clients' lives consistently outperformed the leaders who focused on what was simply in it for the bank. In meetings and conversations with employees, leaders framed the upselling toward job purpose, explaining that they were "helping clients simplify their financial lives and get the best products to meet their needs." Articulated in this way, many of the service reps felt more charged to help their clients and started discussing the other products that they could offer more enthusiastically. Sales increased and so did job engagement.

EXERCISE   *Drive Job Purpose, Not Job Function*

An important shift you can help your employees make is to move from thinking about job function to job purpose. How does the employee's job provide them with more personal meaning, and how does it make a difference to others?

First, make a list of the main job functions in the employee's area of responsibility, with brief descriptions of the role and tasks. Second, brainstorm a big list of ways the job makes a difference: how does it make someone's life, society, or the planet better? Third, craft simple purpose or higher-calling statements. The following are a few examples to get you thinking.

Job Role	Job Function	Job Purpose
Hospital janitor	Clean floors, patient rooms, bathrooms, and offices	Provide a clean, safe, and uncluttered environment to promote patient healing and well-being
Zookeeper	Clean enclosures; feed animals	Contribute to conservation Make animals' lives better Help people learn about nature
Maid	Clean homes	Give people the gift of time Alleviate loneliness

Hotel housekeeper	Set up and clean rooms	Brighten a customer's day
		Ensure that any recyclable waste is recycled
Bank customer service representative	Sell customers banking services and financial products	Simplify customers' lives and provide the best products to meet their needs

GETTING TEAM MEMBERS TO CLAIM THEIR OWN PURPOSE

There is a concept in academic literature called *job crafting*. The idea is that individuals often have a great capacity to design their own jobs in terms of both how they perceive their work and the meaning behind it. People tend to focus on the parts of their job that they find more meaningful overall. Although we appreciate the approach Disney takes in suggesting that every employee at the parks has the same purpose—to spread happiness—our experience has been that helping people identify the specific purpose of their own job is even more powerful in driving purpose.

Several years ago we were working with a large law firm, and each person was going through a process to identify the purpose of their role. The manager at the main office told the receptionist that her purpose was to be the office's "first impressionist" for clients and visitors. He said, "You are the first person our clients interact with when they come to this company, and your impression will tell them what kind of firm we are." The manager had good instincts: the receptionist's function may have been to answer phones and greet people, but her purpose, from the company's perspective, was larger.

The receptionist liked his idea, but when asked what *she* saw as the purpose of her job, she said, "My goal in life is that all day long everyone who meets me gets a shot of positivity. I want them to feel a little better about the world because they met me. My purpose sitting at this desk is to bring more friendliness to the world." At that moment she got visibly excited, saying, "I know I make a first impression for the company, but my job is bigger than that!"

While it's good for leaders to help people discover the purpose of their work, it's even more impactful to have people engage with defining their *own* purpose. You can inspire others with your purpose, values, and mission, or that of the company, but you can't just give someone a purpose. And getting people talking and thinking about job purpose is as, or even more, important than whatever words we ultimately choose to articulate someone's role. Leaders therefore have a dual duty not only to inspire purpose by helping people see beyond the function of their job but also to provide individuals with support to find a way to do that on their own.

As is usually the case, the purpose people arrive at for themselves is much more powerful than the purpose bestowed by someone else. Having conversations with team members about what motivates them and how they define purpose is therefore critical. The more we can help our people and our teams see how their work makes the world better for colleagues, customers, clients, society, and planet, the more we will find a movement toward work becoming a calling throughout the organization.

A simple example may be helpful. We have done a great deal of consulting in the hotel, airline, and hospitality sectors over the past two decades. We vividly recall working with Fairmont Hotels on an initiative to help staff identify the purpose of their jobs. Housekeepers generally found purpose in providing clean rooms, brightening a road warrior's time away from home with a smile or friendly conversation, and acting as the main point of contact for many of the guests after check-in. In other words, their purpose was connected to their direct relationship with customers.

One housekeeper, however, was most excited by the role she played making sure that everything that could be recycled from the rooms she cleaned each day found its way to the recycling bins. "The environment is important to me, as well as my entire family, and this is something I am doing for my children and grandchildren. Knowing that the hotel supports me on this and makes it a priority gives me meaning in my job." This woman took her meaning behind the job—her purpose behind the function—to a new level, one that many people wouldn't necessarily consider. She connected her job with her family well-being and the overall state of the environment, and her bosses and managers supported her wholeheartedly.

One of the more interesting ways to help others find their purpose came to us from John Viera, global director of sustainability at Ford Motor Company. As part of its efforts to engage team members in sustainability and Ford's purpose to create a better world, the company sent out a survey, asking employees to identify how they were contributing to sustainability in their current roles. We loved this method because rather than simply tell people how they were contributing, it enables team members to claim and name that which is already present and meaningful to them in their work. We recommend that leaders conduct similar surveys to help employees crystalize what is meaningful to them in their positions. In so doing you facilitate a connection to their job purpose, over job function, and you learn more about their approach to purpose.

For leaders the question becomes *Do we help people see how their day-to-day work is both contributing to a better world, society, and planet, as well as better lives for our customers?* As we have said many times so far, the more people are directly involved in answering those questions for themselves, the better; but leaders must *model* job purpose by speaking regularly about their own purpose, help team members frame work toward purpose rather than function, and ask questions that help each person uncover their own purpose.

HELPING PEOPLE FIND THEIR "JOB FIT"

As stated, research shows that there are two key elements to perceiving a job as a calling. The first is seeing how the job serves a purpose, often in the form of some meaningful contribution to colleagues, customers, society, or the planet. The second involves something we call *job fit*. That is, does a person feel that the tasks of their daily job align with their talents and personal gifts? One way to think about the difference is comparing the outcome of the tasks we perform (e.g., the gift of time, alleviating loneliness) with the moment-to-moment experience of the particular tasks (e.g., housecleaning), which we call *craft*.

For example, one physician we worked with serves as a great example of both purpose and craft. After having practiced cardiology for many years, he decided to take a senior administrative position. Although he had a deep sense of purpose in helping the entire health system serve patients more effectively, he missed the enjoyment of solving specific clinical problems. That process had given him a true sense of calling, one that he often found lacking in his new leadership role. The problem was about job fit, and we discussed ways that he could address the issue. We first talked about his current job functions and the purpose he found behind them. Then we discussed what he felt his strong points were as a physician and the tasks he enjoyed. Throughout our dialogue we brainstormed how he could fulfill both elements.

After our meeting he decided to involve himself in a weekly clinical roundup with physicians in his area of expertise. In these meetings a large group of cardiologists would discuss particularly vexing clinical cases in an effort to develop solutions. By spending just one hour per week in those meetings, helping solve the clinical puzzles of a few cases, his work as an administrator gained new meaning and he reconnected to his calling. By connecting both elements—purpose and fit—he truly felt that he was doing the work he was meant to do.

To help your team members focus on their calling, talk with them about both purpose and craft. Discuss what tasks or aspects of the job give them the most meaning; then help them find ways to make that part of the job more present for them. You can have these discussions formally or informally—in whichever setting you believe the person will be most comfortable. In the process you'll get to form a closer bond and connection and better understand their motivations. You should also share your own personal purpose and how you think it relates to the company's mission and long-term goals. Help your team members see that you too are intent on finding a calling, and show how you've been able to work toward that within the organization.

EXERCISE	*Talk to Your Team*

There is nothing wrong with informal conversations with individual team members about their values and purpose, but if you want to show that you're serious about purpose—and helping people connect with it personally—holding a more formal team meeting is an excellent approach.

- Start by explaining the difference between job function and job purpose.

- Then discuss the job functions the team performs. Have them identify these functions and write them down on a whiteboard or other visible place in the meeting room.

- Next, talk about the purpose behind each of those functions. Ask for input from every individual in the room if possible.

- Write the purpose next to the function.

From there start to narrow the conversation by asking which purposes people feel most connected to. See if there are any others that should be included. You will find that some team members are on board with a greater purpose, but they feel that their talents are not being used most effectively.

Some team members may enjoy certain tasks that others don't, so get them to talk about that and see if you can better delegate work based on this discussion. This type of meeting draws on helping others find, and name, their individual and team purpose and their appropriate job fit to connect everyone more with a calling as compared with "just another job."

THE HIGHER PURPOSE OF PUB FOOD

Even CEOs can experience a shift from job function to job purpose that is transformative for their own work and ultimately their organization. One of our former clients was Applebee's, a leading restaurant chain with more than 2,000 casual outlets worldwide. Lloyd Hill became the CEO in 1997, and during his decade of leadership the company grew significantly in both market share and profitability. Hill told us a story about his first months as an executive at Applebee's:

> I went out to visit scores of our restaurants just to get close to the operation. As I visited the different outlets, I noticed a pattern.
>
> In some of the restaurants, people remembered customers' names and knew their favorite dishes. Staff members treated one another with a visible positive attitude, and they were directly involved in doing good things in the community—engaging with charitable efforts, from participating in cancer marches to helping the homeless. At other outlets the opposite was true. They didn't remember your name or your favorite dish, staff members were not particularly nice to each other, and they were not involved in the community.
>
> After I left some of the restaurants, I felt a little better about the world, and after leaving others I felt a little worse.

As Hill contemplated this difference, he wrote down a simple phrase: *At Applebee's we are in the business of making people's lives a little better for the hour they spend in our restaurants.* The focus moved him from job function (we sell food) to job purpose (we make people's lives better). The shift made a huge difference for Hill personally and would later become a key part of the CEO's communication to staff and leaders. Over time Hill and his senior team took this simple idea to drive higher engagement through a purpose bigger than selling food. Though Hill could not directly attribute to this shift Applebee's growth to become the most successful chain in the casual-dining space during his tenure, he felt that by driving purpose the energy in the organization improved palpably.

The topmost leader's work can be transformed when we see the higher purpose of work, the way it becomes a calling. Applebee's grew mightily during that decade of Hill's service, and knowing what we do about purpose, this should come as no surprise. Whether it is the CEO or the most frontline person, this movement toward job purpose and away from mere job function is how great companies will not only thrive in the purpose revolution but bring new sources of meaning and vitality to every team member.

EACH OF US CAN MOVE OUR COMPANY TOWARD PURPOSE

Of course, many of you are thinking, *But I am not the CEO; what if my company doesn't have the kind of inspiring purpose that I hope for? Or what if the purpose is there, but it's dormant? What influence do I really have on my company?* We think the story of Ray Andersen, who is a kind of folk hero in sustainable business circles, is particularly instructive.

After university Andersen founded Interface Carpets, which would become the largest producer of modular carpeting in the world, with sales in 110 countries. He is most famous, however, for his efforts to promote environmentally friendly practices, including a quest for zero waste and zero emissions. Not only does his company remain a sustainability leader since his death in 2011 but he personally inspired thousands of other leaders to take the cause of doing good in business much more seriously.

Now before you think, *Okay, one more story about the impact of a CEO,* it is worthwhile to explore how Ray became a champion and what set Interface down the path of purpose for a better future. Though the story goes that he read a book by a colleague of ours, Paul Hawken, who wrote *The Ecology of Commerce: A Declaration of Sustainability,* the real question is, *Why did he even bother to read that book?*

In the mid-1990s some of Interface's large customers started asking its salespeople about how sustainable its carpets were, what happened to the waste in its factories, and how much of it was recycled. A group of those sales leaders decided that Interface needed a sustainability plan and asked Andersen if they could form a working group. With the CEO's blessing, they also asked if he would come to their first meeting and share his personal "sustainability vision."

By his own admission, Andersen had never really given any thought to environmental sustainability; but he set out on a quest, which included reading Hawken's book, and the rest, as they say, is history. Those few salespeople who asked to form a working group not only launched the CEO's journey but ultimately served as the genesis for one of the most successful purpose-focused companies of our time. Their names were not long remembered, but their impact is undeniable!

So, you may not be the CEO, but when each of us thinks of our job purpose and not just our job function, we can influence in ways we can hardly imagine.

BEST PRACTICES FOR
DRIVING PURPOSE

- Take the initiative to talk about job purpose over job function. When you discuss purpose honestly and openly, your team and colleagues are more likely to relate to the stated purpose. It takes courage, but the outcomes can be astounding.

- To connect employees with their job purpose, directly explain the greater value they provide, not just the tasks they need to perform. Reiterate this value in group and one-on-one meetings, during performance reviews, and when discussing new projects or initiatives.

- Make a table that lists job role, function, and purpose to help uncover and better articulate the purpose behind the function for your employees, both as a team and as individuals.

- Inspire others with your or the company's purpose, values, and mission—but help them discover and define their own.

- Help people find their calling at work. Learn about their values and aspirations and what drives meaning for them; then provide them with jobs, roles, assignments, and volunteer opportunities that connect to their sense of purpose.

- Have employees imagine the higher purpose of their job and tasks, and then focus on how what they do makes a difference for customers, society, and the planet.

- Have workshops or discussions with your team to connect their work to higher purpose in their own words.

CHAPTER 7

Get Hands-On Purpose

F OR MANY YEARS JOHN WAS A REGULAR KEYNOTE SPEAKER AT THE annual Inc. 500 conferences, where the 500 fastest-growing privately held companies gathered. In the mid-1990s, shortly after *Awakening Corporate Soul* was published, the socially responsible business movement was just getting started in a serious way. After John's talk one year, the CEO of an up-and-coming retailer asked him a question about an experience the CEO had had with his employees.

"We are a very socially responsible business," the CEO told John. "We give a great deal away to charity, we have a great set of values, we care about our people, and we offer an amazing product to our customers. Last month a group of 50 employees volunteered together to work with inner-city kids. People came back buzzing and engaged like I have never seen them before. How do you think I can get that kind of energy back at the office?"

His question was important, and it's related to an issue that we have experienced with many organizations over the years. His company was doing many of the right things: it had a purpose, it was generous, it was good to its customers and employees—and yet something was missing. As John probed more deeply, he soon discovered that most of the purpose-related activities in the company were headed up by the senior leaders. Aside from the volunteer day, the majority of the purpose-oriented work they were doing was in the form of charitable donations.

The company's values and mission were inspiring, but when John asked how much employees got to shape those values, how involved they were on a day-to-day basis with the company's social mission, and how much influence they had in deciding where the company donated money, the CEO shrugged and said, "Well, they don't."

His employees felt remote and isolated from the process—and rightfully so. My advice to him was simple: "Get your people more involved. Get their hands on your purpose. Right now, the purpose is yours, and you need to find a way to make them feel like it's theirs."

Traditionally, as discussed earlier, businesses have tried to activate purpose in a top-down way: the leaders determined the mission and values and then disseminated them to the people. The company decided what philanthropic efforts it would support, but most of that was in the form of ceremoniously handing a check to the chosen charity. Employees may have been encouraged to donate a small portion of their salary to well-known charities like the United Way, and customers were the passive receptors for one-way advertising messages about the company's philanthropy.

We are not saying that charitable giving is not important, nor that there aren't times when a company must act without wide consent of its stakeholders, but thriving in the age of social good requires new thinking. Today's talent, and customers as well, are eager to get involved, get their hands dirty, and feel that they are directly contributing to making a better society and planet. They want to help shape a company's values and take part in decisions about where it focuses its efforts to change the world. Employees also want the workplace to help them participate in this change.

This is an important shift. In the past, if an organization was seen as doing good, employees and customers were happy to sit on the sidelines. In the purpose revolution, they want to be on the front lines. Your team members want to help shape your company's purpose and values, and your customers want to work with you to make a better world. We call this shift *from bystander to participant,* and to thrive in the age of social good, leaders need to find ways to get what we call *hands-on purpose*.

FROM BYSTANDER TO PARTICIPANT

The shift from bystander to participant has major ramifications as it's taking place across society, with business in that larger context. Millennials, certainly in North America, have grown up with a much more egalitarian parenting style than did the previous generation. In part as a reaction to the more "because I said so" approach of their own parents, the baby boomers involved their children in negotiating their lives to a large extent. A casual observation of parents with their children in the grocery store, debating which cereal to buy, is witness to the change that has occurred.

The same is true of schools in North America. Almost every baby boomer has a story about a friend in Catholic school, suffering the proficient aim of a ruler in the hands of a stern nun. By contrast, their children often negotiated with their teachers the criteria for the success of projects. From the ability to choose whatever you want from a million options online (books, movies, music, groceries, clothes—the list goes on!), to a world where social media invites us to regularly connect and interact with people at any time, to open-door policies at companies in which leaders are regularly accessible and often called by their first name—this shift from bystander to participant is happening everywhere. We can argue about the merits of more-participatory parents, schools, and business environments, but it would be hard to argue that people today don't expect to be involved! The observer age is obsolescent.

Developing countries have also experienced this shift, as seen in the Arab Spring that swept across the Middle East in 2010 or simply the increasing ability to connect in a nanosecond with anyone in the world. Today's employees and customers no longer wish to sit on the sidelines; they are eager to get involved. Organizations that are truly thriving in this new world are practicing hands-on purpose.

Team members are helping shape a company's mission, values, and purpose—and are being offered ways to get their hands dirty at work in making a difference—and both employees and customers have a say in how companies engage to make a better world.

MAKE INVOLVEMENT YOUR PASSION

Companies need to constantly look for ways to engage team members directly in efforts to make society better and to define the company's values and goals on such issues. It is important that companies have lofty visions about making an impact on large issues, such as climate change and poverty, but unless your team feels that they are directly part of a meaningful effort to make the world better, purpose will fall flat.

Emzingo cofounder and managing partner Drew Bonfiglio has a bird's-eye view of the emerging purpose-focused employee. His company designs programs for young talent to experience meaningful work both within and outside the company. One example is the company's work with Everis, a Spanish information technology (IT) consulting firm. Emzingo designed and facilitated a series of workshops with Everis for its high-potential employees and managers in training. One two-day workshop was based on action learning and using social impact as a vehicle for practical learning to find meaning and purpose in their jobs.

By connecting with local field partners, including NGOs, nonprofits, and community-based organizations, Emzingo identified challenges that these employees could confront. Employees then used their prior experience and new knowledge from the workshop to find solutions to these challenges. In these types of programs, participants are encouraged to regularly reflect on the role of business, how social innovation can have a positive impact on business, and how their individual roles in an organization can have meaning and purpose.

Bonfiglio told us that when people feel empowered and excited by Emzingo programs, they often get "really frustrated" when they return to work and their companies or leaders don't understand how important purpose is to them. He also explained that when people get to be involved in projects that make a difference, it not only engages them but also makes them hungry to replicate the experience at their jobs. He emphasized that younger employees want it *all* at work: they want to have a great career *and* feel that they are getting to make a difference in a hands-on way. He told us, "These guys just don't want to settle."

At 3M sustainability has increasingly become core to the company's mission, and team members there tell us that this emerging focus is deeply motivating. The emerging company purpose centers around the concept of *improving every life*. It is expressed in a three-part mantra: *3M technology advancing every company, 3M products enhancing every home, and 3M innovation improving every life.* On its website 3M communicates the inspiring nature of its purpose: "Improving every life is an exciting endeavor and an ambitious one. It's the right thing to do and core to who we are." But improving the planet and every life, which is central to its core purpose, must include ways for team members to get their hands on that purpose.

Historically, 3M is famous for granting employees 15 percent of their time to work on creative projects of their choosing. That time is increasingly being spent on purpose projects related to a sustainable future. Jean Bennington Sweeney, 3M's chief sustainability officer, says, "One of the things we are working toward is helping each function see their role in sustainability—not just the people who have *sustainability* in their titles."

Among other activities, 3M holds a Sustainability Week that involves workshops and contests to successfully engage employees around the globe. One competition includes developing ideas for sustainable solutions to major problems. Teams compete, and the winners present their ideas to a panel of senior executives, including the CEO, senior vice president of research and development (R&D), chief marketing officer, and chief sustainability officer. Employees vote for their favorite idea—whether it relates directly to products and services or to corporate programs—and the winners get marketing and R&D funding to put their plan into action.

Winning product and program ideas have been in areas ranging from road safety, to energy production, to human health. Through this program 3M sends a clear message: every person in the company is a sustainability leader and can truly make a difference. In other words, you as a team member are at the center of purpose, not merely observing it.

Like 3M, German company Henkel AG & Co. has made sustainability core to its business: "'Creating sustainable value' is our purpose that unites all of us at Henkel."[1] As a company that proactively seeks ways to activate its purpose in the workplace, society, and the environment, Henkel strives to "balance between people, planet and profit" and takes a "long-term, entrepreneurial approach toward all elements of sustainability, aiming not just to comply with existing standards but also to shape new ones." A commitment to sustainability has always been "a major driver" of its success.

But how does Henkel make these ideals practical in the real world? In a 2014 interview with McKinsey & Company, then Henkel CEO Kasper Rorsted shed some light on this question: "Many companies have sustainability strategies and targets, but sustainability can only become an integral part of people's daily work if all employees understand the underlying principles. When I am asked how many employees are working on sustainability at Henkel, I always reply: 47,000. Each employee has the responsibility, and each makes a contribution. But in order to do this, they need to know and understand our strategy."[2]

Rorsted went on to describe the importance of getting everyone engaged around sustainability. The company sponsored workshops for its 2030 sustainability strategy, where "managers at all levels and their teams developed a sustainability action plan for their own particular areas." In all, the company conducted 670 workshops around the world, "which yielded around 6,000 initiatives for implementation."

One notable outcome of these workshops was "the idea of supporting employees to become 'sustainability ambassadors.'" Their role is to be proactive, to "talk about sustainability to coworkers, suppliers, customers, and students." They also provide sustainability classes and visit schools—and their results have been impressive. According to Rorsted, "We have trained more than 1,300 sustainability ambassadors, and more than 6,700 children in 23 countries have attended a sustainability session."

EXERCISE *Engage Your Team in Hands-On Purpose*

No matter the size of your company, these types of programs and activities are not difficult to implement. Here are just some of the things you can do as a leader:

- Host an annual competition or announce a well-timed new initiative to help employees not only think about purpose but also come up with actual ways to infuse it in the company.

- Give employees free time to brainstorm how they personally, and the company collectively, can attack issues of sustainability, corporate and social responsibility, and environmental awareness. If they have a great idea that's possible to put into place, don't wait—do it!

- Involve your employees in deciding where your charitable giving goes. In fact, involve your customers as well.

- Sponsor an Annual Day of Giving or something similar for team members to volunteer on a regular basis.

- Set up a community board in the major areas you serve. Engage these boards to direct where philanthropic contributions and volunteer efforts should go to have maximum impact.

▓ Enroll "champions" to develop or lead grassroots
  efforts to support corporate social responsibility (CSR)
  initiatives and goals.

▓ Dedicate a percentage of time each year for employees
  to volunteer or do community work.

▓ Develop formal social intern programs or service corps
  to give employees an opportunity to address socioeconomic problems in your communities.

▓ Form partnerships with customers, NGOs, government,
  and other businesses to work together on common
  socioeconomic or environmental problems. Give
  employees opportunities to lead and participate in
  these partnerships. Have them report back to the organization to give presentations, including videos and
  testimonials about their experiences and the results
  they saw.

▓ Encourage each team member to commit to one or two
  programs or activities each year.

Volunteering Pays Twice

To close the purpose gap and help employees get their hands-on
purpose, it's necessary to support and advocate for their personal
enrichment through contributing to others' well-being. Employees
want to work for a company that makes a positive impact on the world,
one that offers programs where they can join with colleagues to tackle
local or global challenges. It's not enough to simply say your company
believes in the important social or environmental issues of the day. You
must demonstrate involvement, both within the company and outside,
and make sure your employees have the chance to be a part of it.

　　Forbes Insights reported in 2011 that 60 percent of companies
surveyed agreed with the statement *Philanthropy and volunteerism are
critical for recruiting younger qualified employees.*[3] Developing in-house
volunteer programs, allowing sabbaticals for volunteer opportunities,

and setting up social and community events are just a few ways to enable your employees to get involved with issues that they care about.

The purpose revolution has renegotiated the social contract between company and employee, expanding beyond the transactional pay for time and output contract. Employee learning and development programs are undergoing radical changes as companies realize the value of nonjob experiences, such as community enrichment and volunteer programs.

For example, Cisco's global program, Time2Give, provides employees 40 hours of volunteer time annually—paid! This time does not come out of their other vacation days or paid time off. In addition, volunteer events are often part of Cisco's offsite meetings, as the company considers "giving back" as part of its DNA. In 2015 employees gave more than 155,000 hours of volunteer time to nonprofits or causes that they individually chose.[4] That year Cisco posted revenue earnings of $49.2 billion.[5]

A purpose organization case study by LinkedIn demonstrates how one popular microfinance company, Kiva, gives employees an opportunity to make a difference outside of work while also learning more about how the company directly affects its customers. Kiva's mission is *to connect people through lending to alleviate poverty.* Most people join Kiva to help others, but with the company operating a digital platform with lenders and clients around the world, that experience could get lost. Instead, Kiva makes a deliberate effort to weave impact into the employee experience.

Every other year Kiva funds an international trip for each employee to travel to a client and directly experience Kiva's impact. When they return, employees formally share the experience with their colleagues. This practice yields a constant stream of powerful stories. Each employee's trip is repeated every second year to keep the emotional connection between work and purpose alive.[6]

Companies find that volunteering pays twice. It not only is a key attractor for top talent in a competitive labor market but also helps improve the health and vitality of the workforce. Studies show that 78 percent of people who volunteered in the past year reported lower stress levels, 76 percent said that volunteering has made them feel healthier, and volunteers report coming back as better leaders and performers.[7] Millennials are especially keen on philanthropy and social participation. One survey found that most—63 percent—gave to charities, 43 percent actively volunteered or were a member of a community organization, and 52 percent signed petitions.[8]

How One Leader Turned Purpose to Profit

Giving people a chance to get hands-on purpose can have a large positive impact on a company, or even a team, regardless of size or scale. Take Deb Elliott, who years ago took over a high-profile retail outlet of The Body Shop on Robson Street in Vancouver. The store was performing quite poorly in terms of sales, and the staff weren't all that engaged. When Elliott took over as store manager, she could have focused on sales, prodding her team members to win more customers. Instead she took time to find out what causes her young staff members cared about most deeply. Soon it became apparent that raising awareness of the then expanding AIDS epidemic was something everyone on her staff could get behind.

The team started volunteering together, and the more they got involved in making a difference, the more deeply engaged they became in the store as a source of meaning. Sales grew steadily, and the store moved from a chronic underperformer to a high performer on business results during Elliott's tenure. This story is a great example of your not needing to be the CEO to reap the benefits of hands-on purpose. It also shows that a good way to engage people on the path of purpose can often be unrelated to the core business. Elliott discovered that when you get people engaged in making a difference, their overall commitment to the business grows.

Facilitating volunteer opportunities for your employees gives them exciting new learning experiences and the chance to take action, directly confronting a societal ill or issue that they care about. It also shows customers and investors that you care about more than the bottom line and that you're willing to lead your team in the right direction. Today no one wants to work for or buy from a soulless, faceless corporation. You need to highlight your company's efforts to effect positive change or you risk becoming irrelevant and missing out on the success of those companies wholeheartedly embracing the purpose revolution.

HANDS-ON PURPOSE AT IBM

When we interviewed Jen Crozier, the vice president of corporate citizenship at IBM and the president of the IBM Foundation, she told us that "paycheck philanthropy is out; involvement is in. I speak at a lot of universities, and students tell us, 'Don't just give me an opportunity to give some of my paycheck; give me a chance to get involved in making a difference.'" With that dynamic in mind, IBM established the Corporate Service Corps, a pristine example of getting hands-on purpose.

The program selects top management prospects and then trains and dispatches these leaders-to-be to emerging markets around the world. Participants spend four weeks in groups of 10 to 15, helping solve economic and social problems of their selected community. Teams work collaboratively with their government and community counterparts to implement socially responsible business practices with measurable results in a global context.

The IBM Corporate Service Corps shows how purpose can drive many different benefits all at the same time. The most obvious benefit is directly to the participants. People we have met who get to be part of these kinds of programs often find them life changing, and they cement their relationship with the company. Serving alongside deeply engaged colleagues is rewarding itself, but doing so while associating your work with making the world better is invaluable. Employees appreciate the company's providing them with meaningful time that would otherwise be used for normal, day-to-day duties. In the process, team members learn firsthand about the emerging markets and can help the company tailor its services to those communities, and they gain new skills in leading from a global perspective.

According to IBM, since its launch in 2008 the service corps has had a positive impact on the lives of more the 140,000 people, by helping communities learn new skills and build their capacity to take action on their own in the future. The program has sent more than 4,000 participants on 250-plus teams to more than 40 countries. Participants hail from over 60 countries and have served communities in Argentina, Brazil, Cambodia, Chile, China, Colombia, Egypt, Ethiopia, Ghana, India, Indonesia, Kazakhstan, Kenya, Malaysia, Mexico, Morocco, Nigeria, Peru, the Philippines, Poland, Romania, Russia, Senegal, South Africa, Sri Lanka, Taiwan, Tanzania, Thailand, Tunisia, Turkey, Vietnam, the United Arab Emirates, and Ukraine. The program continues to expand to new locations each year.[9]

Crozier says that this program, and others like it at IBM, "are like helium for employees, lifting all the metrics such as engagement; it develops leadership skills, and 90 percent of those who have participated in the service corps call it one of the best development experiences of their lifetime." She says that thousands compete for the 500 slots available each year.

IBM says that the turnover rate for team members who take part in the program is basically zero. Having associated making a hands-on difference with their employment at IBM, the relationship between participants and the company becomes profoundly deeper. Not every person in a company can be sent on such a mission, but even the chance to potentially do so, and the knowledge that your company is performing such important work, augments the overall goodwill that employees associate with the company. As one IBM'er said to us, "This whole idea of 'creating a smarter planet' makes me proud to be part of this company."

At IBM employees and retirees can also take advantage of less ambitious efforts, including volunteering at a school or community organization for kids and connecting with other participants on the future of volunteer service. The idea, Crozier says, "is to give people a menu of opportunities, then let them choose."

Whether it involves volunteering for a day of service or a long-term project, helping shape the values of the company, working in a soup kitchen, having time on the company's dime to brainstorm sustainability ideas or to be a champion of sustainability—the point is that making society better can't just be something the *company* does. You need to find a way to help your people get hands-on purpose. In the process, you'll also develop ideas for involving your customers directly, as well.

IBM earns a great amount of goodwill among potential customers in the communities and countries it serves through the Corporate Service Corps and other programs. In addition to connecting with your employees over purpose, you need to connect with your customers as well, showing them how you're making an effort to effect change but also providing ways for them to get their hands on purpose as well.

EXERCISE *Establishing Volunteer Programs and Opportunities*

Establishing and facilitating volunteer opportunities may be even easier than you think. The following are some actions that you and your team can take.

- Have your team brainstorm a list of connections your company already has with the community or any type of charitable organization, local, regional, domestic, or international.

- Contact local leaders, community centers, and program administrators and see how you might be able to work together on an issue they're currently facing.

- Speak with your employees about the causes and organizations that they might be personally invested in. Ask them how they think they could use their talents to help those groups.

Unlike Cisco, not every company is willing and able to provide employees with 40 hours a year for volunteer opportunities; but providing your employees with a day or two every business quarter won't disrupt their flow of work and will enable and inspire them to get involved. If possible, use these volunteer experiences to show employees how their everyday work affects the surrounding community and beyond. It is an excellent use of their time and the company's time. Like with Kiva, employees' experiencing the direct impact of their work will not only have them returning to the job energized but also help keep that excitement alive.

Such volunteer programs also help individual team members develop their leadership skills. The following are ways to connect volunteering to leadership skills and employee development.

- Identify knowledge, skills, or abilities that you wish to develop in your team.

- Identify potential leaders or star performers based on past experience and current performance.

- Have a one-on-one meeting about what causes they're interested in, and then help them connect directly with an organization doing this type of work.

- Document the volunteer experiences as leadership or employee development in performance reviews just as you would other types of development activities.

Employees will appreciate your willingness to help them get involved, and they'll gain hands-on experience in a new field. Volunteering also gives them real-world skills in working with others and leading with purpose.

JOIN HANDS WITH YOUR CUSTOMERS

In the purpose revolution, it is more critical than ever to engage your customers in the same way you involve your team members. When focusing on social good efforts, always ask, *How can we work with our customers to make a difference?* This is a profound shift from simply asking, *How can we show our customers we are making a difference?*

Involving customers in such efforts, however, is a novel concept for many companies, and they may not realize how much careful planning is required. Most importantly, the effort must be connected to your core mission and be implemented strategically.

Pepsi made headlines in 2010 when it abandoned its buy of Super Bowl ads and instead ran its Refresh campaign, in which it gave away $20 million to charities based on consumer nominations. The campaign was well intentioned and generated lots of news before and after the game. Pepsi directly reached out to customers and potential customers to get them involved, providing a way for their voices to be heard and their chosen charities to be supported.

Yet the reviews of the campaign's success were quite mixed. First, there was voter confusion over the process. Second, having people nominate charities and crowd-source votes is fraught with all kinds of dangers, such as having charities nominated that your company, or a large number of customers, may not approve of. Ballot stuffing, so to speak, is also an issue, as charities can rally people to vote for their cause. Pepsi also didn't connect with a charity related to its core mission or purpose. As result, customers couldn't necessarily connect Pepsi with a specific cause, either. Without that connection, the campaign appeared to many observers as forced or disingenuous.

Pepsi also cast a wide net regarding the audience. It's good to involve as many people as possible, but it's more important to know your customers and how they'll approach such a campaign. The company's instincts were good, but if you recall the Seventh Generation toxic chemicals effort discussed in chapter 1, you'll see an instructive comparison.

In the case of the toxic chemicals campaign, it was 100 percent aligned with Seventh Generation's brand and purpose. The full-page ad in the *New York Times* felt authentic and was focused on engaging the very kinds of customers that the company aimed at winning over and getting involved. The act of signing a petition was simple and straightforward, lending itself to little confusion about what the company was trying to accomplish and how customers could help.

The Pepsi campaign's execution was confusing for customers, who were unclear on the voting process. The campaign also failed to focus on core issues that Pepsi was tackling. And while it caught headlines (BIG COMPANY FOREGOES ADS IN FAVOR OF MAKING A DIFFERENCE), it lacked a strategic connection to the company's purpose. Without that kind of focus, such efforts fail to truly engage people in getting their hands-on purpose.

Contrast this with a 2017 video produced by Heineken in the United Kingdom focused on building bridges.[10] The video featured real people, with fundamentally different viewpoints on such issues as feminism and climate change, who were put together and given a task to build a bridge together. Once the task was completed, they showed participants videos of the person they built the bridge with, expressing views diametrically opposed to their own. They were then given the option to sit down and have a beer together to talk about their differences or leave the room. Unlike the Pepsi campaign, this video had no celebrities, did not focus on the product, and connected to a deeply felt issue of our time: the capacity to have authentic conversations to bridge our differences.

It's a great feeling for executives, leaders, and employees when the right campaign is properly executed, helping customers get their hands-on purpose and having a direct impact on a cause they care about. But it also contributes to the company's success—remember, doing good has become good business. To maintain that feeling and success, however, a new type of company has been gaining popularity since the mid-2000s. This model is sometimes known as *one-to-one* and is based on the idea that every time a customer buys a product, the company donates the same product to a person in need, typically in a developing country. Let's take a look at one company following this model, doing great work and performing extremely well.

The Warby Parker Story

Warby Parker, the online eyewear provider, is a great entrepreneurial success. When founded in 2010, like so many businesses it sought to solve a real problem: figure out how to manufacture and sell affordable, fashionable glasses. This is how the company tells its founding story:

> Every idea starts with a problem. Ours was simple: glasses are too expensive. We were students when one of us lost his glasses on a backpacking trip. The cost of replacing them was so high that he spent the first semester of grad school without them, squinting and complaining. (We don't recommend this.) The rest of us had similar experiences, and we were amazed at how hard it was to find a pair of great frames that didn't leave our wallets bare. Where were the options?
>
> It turns out there was a simple explanation. The eyewear industry is dominated by a single company that has been able to keep prices artificially high while reaping huge profits from consumers who have no other options.
>
> We started Warby Parker to create an alternative.[11]

The company's first purpose was to help customers access high-end eyeglasses at a lower cost (recall the primary purpose of all businesses discussed in chapter 2). But the founders also knew that more than a billion people globally don't have access to eyeglasses, meaning 15 percent of the planet is at a disadvantage in both work and life (recall that a commitment to society and the world is the second purpose). So, from the very start, Warby Parker collaborated with a nonprofit called VisionSpring. The idea was simple and easy to understand: for every pair of glasses sold each month, the company would contribute an amount to VisionSpring, resulting in that same number of glasses being distributed to people in need around the globe.

Warby Parker doesn't physically donate a pair of glasses. Through VisionSpring, local people are trained to conduct low-cost exams and sell ultra-affordable eyewear, thus meeting the need for glasses and enabling new small businesses in developing countries. Customers receive an inexpensive high-quality product and directly contribute to two important causes: eye care and job creation in places that may have few opportunities for either.

This is a prime example of hands-on purpose with customers. It is simple, it is fully integrated with the product itself, and customers can see how their purchases directly involve them in the company's efforts to make a better world. Warby Parker also claims to be carbon neutral, and though that's excellent, it is unlikely to attract and retain customers in the same way its main purpose does. While being carbon neutral is important and even critical to the planet, the eyewear one-for-one is something customers can get their hands on and feel like *I am part of this. The company's purpose is my purpose too.*

Though this model may be easier to implement in start-ups or new organizations, it's still a viable approach for new initiatives, products, or services at large, well-established companies. For example, if your company is launching a new product, consider how you can connect its purchase with a charitable donation or cause. You don't need to rewrite the whole playbook of your company's processes, supply chain, or distribution; you just need to come up with a way to help your customers help others by using your product or service. Remember that it must relate to your core values, mission, and purpose as an organization. Without that authenticity, your customer won't connect to the cause.

EXERCISE   *Make Your Customers' Cause Your Cause*

As you think about involving your customers in your purpose, ask your team, employees, colleagues, and leaders these important questions:

- What are our customers' core values?
- What do they believe in the most?
- What change or good do they want to see in the world?

Then there are these questions to consider:

- How can we help further their cause?
- How does this align with our values and what we believe in?

■ How can we go the extra step to provide a connection between customer action and visible results, such as with the one-to-one approach?

After developing a few ideas based on these questions and conversations, reach out to your customers to take their pulse. Obviously, social media plays a major role in connecting with customers and their opinions.

You might consider having the marketing department conduct a Facebook survey to poll your current followers. When using a social media platform for which you have already built a following, you'll be connecting with people that most likely currently use your products and services.

Instead of casting a net that's simply too wide, focus on your customers and find out what's important to them, what they consider their contribution to the greater good, and what you can do to connect them with a meaningful cause to get their hands-on purpose.

The TELUS Transformation

TELUS, the Canadian telecommunications company based in Vancouver, has embraced the idea of hands-on purpose to significant benefit. The process began when CEO Darren Entwistle first came on board. Since he joined the team almost 20 years ago, TELUS has been one of the most profitable telecommunications companies in the world. It also has among the highest employee engagement numbers of any company of its size and composition. Under Entwistle's leadership, TELUS has staked its reputation on leading the drive for social good and has won numerous awards and distinctions for being socially and environmentally responsible.

Entwistle, like Steve Jobs, is a bit paradoxical. He can be very tough, does not suffer fools, and is unabashed in communicating how great his company is. But his passion for the business and for the role that social good plays both in the success of TELUS and the good it can do for society is off the charts. An hour talking to Entwistle about purpose and what it means for both his company and the world leaves one ready to join the revolution.

"We have three great pillars of challenge and opportunity that face us as a society," he told us, "environment, education, and health care. We need to do something about all three of these things. We need a sustainable environment, we need opportunity for equal access to education for a broader group of people, and we need to meet the growing health-care challenges at a cost we can afford." He is unequivocal that he sees TELUS playing a critical role in solving these issues, and this idea permeates the company culture.

Sandy McIntosh is the executive vice president of people and culture and the chief HR officer at TELUS; she sums it up when she says, "Every day our team members across the country are improving the lives of Canadians and the communities in which they live. Giving back is in our DNA—it's core to our values and at the heart of our culture." TELUS team members also told us that Entwistle's personal sense of purpose around the company's true purpose have motivated them to find personal purpose in their work.

When Entwistle joined the company in 2000, he launched an effort to define a new set of company values. The senior team could have gone off and written the values on their own, but instead he commissioned an internal effort to ask thousands of employees what values they held personally and what they felt made TELUS great. The core set of values that emerged from that process has stood the test of time. More importantly, the tone was set from the get-go that *These values are ours!*

TELUS leaders then focused on how they could give team members opportunities to directly serve society and causes they care about. One of their most successful efforts is the TELUS Day of Giving, an annual effort where the company, over a period of about a month, sources out opportunities for team members to volunteer (and bring their families and friends along too). Employees volunteer in community programs that are building schools, improving parks, and supporting local hospitals. Team members have volunteered more than 6 million hours, performing the work on their own time, often on the weekend.

"We have measured it, and team members who participate in the Day of Giving opportunities are more engaged at work," says Jill Schnarr, vice president of community affairs at TELUS. The company's employee engagement scores are in the high 80s.

The effort works because it moves people from observers or bystanders of purpose to participants. Millennials volunteer on average almost twice as much as their baby boomer counterparts, but two of the biggest barriers to volunteering are time away from family and finding a place to volunteer. TELUS's program removes both barriers. But the company doesn't stop at engaging its employees to get hands-on purpose. It involves customers as well.

TELUS has given about half a billion dollars in philanthropic donations. Before Entwistle such money was granted to charities in the traditional ways of large companies; customers and communities had little say about where those funds were funneled. With Entwistle at the helm, they set up community boards comprising citizens from 12 Canadian regions and five international communities where the company has a large presence. The company empowered these community boards to support grassroots efforts in their respective geographic areas.

This unique approach allows the broader community to feel that they are partners with TELUS in *creating a friendly future*—the company's core mantra. They joined hands with customers when it established the community boards. The shift from *We give* to *You help us decide where to give* bonds customers in new ways.

TELUS has measured customers' views of the company over the years. "We use something called the Omni survey every six months," says Schnarr. "We ask if people know that our company is active in the community and if it influences your decision to continue to do business with us. We used to be at, like, 15 percent; now it is at 50 percent." She adds, "Increasingly, we hear new team members say that one of the reasons they joined the company is because of the work we are doing in the community." Though the TELUS stated purpose is to create a friendly future, it could easily be *Get employees'* and *customers' hands-on purpose.*

Entwistle says that the same principle is at play when matching employee charitable contributions as another way of getting hands-on purpose: "When the focus was just on giving money, of course, people cared; but once we were matching our giving with things our people were already passionate about, engagement went off the charts."

BEST PRACTICES FOR
GETTING HANDS-ON PURPOSE

- Develop competitions, programs, and companywide initiatives to get your employees not only thinking about purpose but coming up with ways to enact it throughout the company.

- Brainstorm all the ways your team can be involved in purpose at work—inside and outside of the company. Encourage each team member to commit to one or two volunteer programs or activities each year.

- Sponsor an annual Day of Giving or something similar for team members to volunteer on a regular basis. Or simply do it with your team.

- Recognize employees for their good works related to sustainability and corporate and social responsibility.

- Develop a one-to-one model within your organization, finding a way for a customer's purchase to directly connect to a worthy cause or charitable donation related to the company's mission and purpose.

- Take the pulse of your customers through a simple social media survey to understand how your campaign or product launch will resonate best with the target audience.

- Establish community boards or other regional committees to support grassroots efforts in deciding how and where to make charitable donations, connecting more directly with customers and their personal purposes and values.

- Recruit champions to develop or lead grassroots efforts to support CSR initiatives and goals.

CHAPTER 8

Create a Clear Line of Sight to Purpose

N 2014 JOHN GAVE TWO KEYNOTE SPEECHES IN SUCCESSIVE WEEKS to two companies in the insurance and financial services industry. Both speeches were at annual meetings headlined by the companies' CEOs, who spoke to their respective top leadership teams, numbering in the hundreds. At the first meeting, the CEO presented a seemingly endless series of slides—there were more than 30 of them, but they could likely have been boiled down to a singular message.

The CEO's main point went something like this: The previous year the company sold more of "everything" and they "sure as hell" had better sell even more the following year. The strategy to implement this plan was unveiled with little emotion or connection to the people the company served other than its shareholders. Though customer service was mentioned here and there, there was no robust discussion of how the company's products or services truly made a difference for anyone, let alone society. When the CEO finished, the applause from the audience was polite but hardly enthusiastic.

John arrived at the meeting of the second company the following week, worried that he might be in for another uninspiring, slide-heavy presentation. This time, though, the CEO had precious few slides. He did talk about the great financial year the company had, but he soon transitioned and said, "Of course, the numbers are not the real story. The real story is that last year we made a difference in the lives of thousands of people and did it with more integrity than anybody else in the business. I am so proud of what we do for people and communities every day."

He then introduced a 12-minute video that featured interviews with the company's clients, ranging from new retirees whose money had been managed, to widows whose husbands' lives had been insured, to employees of organizations who had purchased benefits. Some of the stories were heartwarming; others were heartbreaking, with tearful moments when speaking of loved ones.

John and the other leaders present witnessed the real difference the company made in the lives of real people. When the video was over, the CEO told two personal stories about what the company's values meant to him, and he challenged his leadership team to continue to let the values be a guide in everything they do. "Our success is in our values. It always has been and always will be," he concluded. A rousing standing ovation followed. The impact of the video and the sincerity of the CEO's focus on purpose was tangible. Later that evening at the company dinner, attendees were still buzzing about the video, its authenticity, and the effect it had on them.

We share the story of these two companies to illustrate a key factor to activating purpose inside an organization, something we call *creating a line of sight to purpose*. An objective analysis would show that both companies were making a difference for their customers and society, but the leader of the second company made the connection clear, and the leader of the first company did not. The impact on the engagement of the second company's people was palpable and showed up in their respective engagement scores and customer service performance. Years later the company led without purpose merged with another mediocre brand, and the company with purpose remains a leader in the industry.

Line of sight is about finding consistent ways to help team members, consumers, and investors see the difference your organization is making for both your direct customers and society. In that first meeting John attended, it was obvious that purpose wasn't a priority for the company or its leaders; if it was a priority, they certainly weren't communicating it effectively. In the second meeting, the audience's excitement was energizing. And that's really what you're aiming for— you want your employees, customers, and investors to be exhilarated by your message and enthralled by your purpose, ready to join you in your mission. If they don't understand that mission or can't determine your values and purpose, they won't be willing to unite with you. To foster a purpose-driven culture, you need to create a line of sight to purpose.

WHAT GETS FOCUSED ON GETS DONE

Over the years the well-worn axiom in business *What gets measured gets done* has always given us pause. There is an almost universal belief among businesspeople that if you measure something, it will change. For example, almost every organization measures customer service on a regular basis; some do so almost constantly. Few companies, however, make exponential gains in service performance based on their findings. We think the faith most leaders have in the power of measurement is misplaced. The truth is, what gets *focused on* gets done. What drives change day to day in any company are the things that leaders devote the most attention to, highlight, ask questions about, and discuss with their teams.

A notable example is the Ritz-Carlton, whose purpose is serving guests in an extraordinary way, as stated in its credo: *The Ritz-Carlton Hotel is a place where the genuine care and comfort of our guests is our highest mission.*[1]

One of the ways the Ritz keeps this purpose front and center in each hotel is by holding daily standup briefing meetings. They call these meetings the "lineup," and they occur at the start of every shift in each department at every hotel in the world. The purpose of these meetings—which do indeed happen every day—is to keep line of sight to what really matters. Leaders highlight how team members lived their purpose the previous day or in earlier shifts, remind team members of the real difference they are making for customers, and rotate through the keys to ensuring an amazing guest experience, such as "remembering people's names." The Ritz is not a great service hotel because it measures customer service; it is a leader because every day it focuses on service.

Communicate Purpose Constantly

A great way to begin understanding line of sight is to audit your own communication as a leader and the overall actions of leaders in your organization. What percentage of the communication, questions, and activities are connected to purpose as opposed to profit or task? Changing the mix of messages can have huge impact.

One of the services our company provides is executive coaching, usually with CEOs, business owners, and division presidents. A few years ago, we coached the president of a major division of a large aerospace company. More than 10,000 people reported to her, and she was generally considered a very smart, strategic leader. Yet something was missing. When we interviewed her direct reports and leaders farther down the line, they said that although the president was intelligent and competent, she lacked passion for the company's core purpose of *keeping soldiers safe and maintaining peace for the nation.* Some employees said they felt that the only thing she cared about were the numbers and the shareholders. According to them, she rarely talked about how the company's products and services made a genuine impact on the lives of those they served or on the country.

In our coaching sessions, it was obvious to us that the president cared deeply about the company's purpose, but a purpose audit (the same type we discussed in chapter 3) of both her written and verbal communications did not support that impression. We encouraged her to make one small but significant shift in her regular communications to groups of employees, colleagues, and other leaders: begin with a story about how the company's products and services were helping keep military personnel safe or serving the cause of peace at home and abroad. She worked hard to find real stories of how their technology made a tangible difference, including stories of specific soldiers saved in war zones. We suggested that she focus every day on keeping purpose at the heart of her communications and storytelling.

The main idea was to emphasize the company's mission in almost every group discussion. She would take the same approach in all written communications—purpose first, always. No meaningful communication would lack this focus on purpose. Even when tough decisions needed to be made due to issues like a tightened budget, she needed to insist that the company's actions be positioned around furthering the mission rather than only the shareholders' interests.

Over a six-month period, this small change reaped large benefits, not only for the president's personal leadership brand but also in the overall morale of her division. It became obvious that she cared about results not merely because of the profits but because of how her teams' work had a real impact on their customers and society. Follow-up interviews with her direct reports, as well as objective measures of engagement in her division, showed that employees and other leaders were inspired and energized by the president's stories and newfound focus. Performance increased and so did engagement.

It is not that profits are unimportant—of course they matter. Employees are concerned with the numbers, too, whether profit or other metrics such as a company's market share. But when we focus exclusively on the bottom line, our people lose heart, as do we. We also lose focus on our mission. In chapter 3 we talk about Steve Jobs at Apple and his unrelenting focus on great products over profits. By concentrating on great products, Jobs focused on being of service first, knowing that greater profits were a result of serving—not the other way around. As former president and CEO of Manulife Don Guloien told us, "Most companies start out with that focus," but over time the emphasis shifts more to "shareholders and numbers," and people forget the importance of purpose and service.

To put that focus back where it belongs and build a culture of purpose, leaders at all levels must constantly communicate the company's aspirational purpose and commitment to customers and society. It is helpful to remind yourself before entering a meeting or giving a presentation that the higher purpose should always be present. Think of this fact every single day, especially when you're making critical decisions. How are they in line with your mission and purpose? How can you show your employees how important that purpose is to the company's health and the customers' well-being? Ask yourself: If your company's communication were a movie, does purpose have a starring role or is it merely a supporting actor with occasional lines? Even worse, does purpose just make a cameo appearance?

When you communicate your purpose, you also need to ensure that what you're describing or discussing is relatable for your team members; though your purpose may be global, it must also be explained in the local context. For example, a bank manager at a branch meeting should let team members know about the broader ways the bank is serving its purpose of making life better for customers and society now and in the future. The manager might do this with examples of the company's ongoing efforts to be green or its contributions to an important social cause. These messages and stories must be balanced with the ways that local team members fulfill their purpose day to day.

One branch manager at the Royal Bank of Canada (RBC), that country's largest bank, told us, "I regularly share information at my team meetings about how our company is acting in a way to better society and the planet. But I also try to find simple everyday examples of how we fulfill our purpose. It might be the story of a mortgage approval we got for someone who had been turned down elsewhere or even some kind act a customer service rep in the branch did for an elderly customer. Then I always connect those stories back to our values and our purpose as a company."

At every meeting with associates, leaders should do the following.

- Remind associates of the company's mission and purpose in an authentic way.

- Tell them about the good the company is doing both locally and broadly to make a difference for clients, society, and the planet.

- Suggest ways that your team can live that purpose right after the meeting.

By communicating mission and purpose clearly and consistently, you amplify the contribution your team and employees make to a noble higher purpose. Don't limit yourself either—try to think of new ways to amplify and communicate purpose every day. For example, we worked with one manager who had a wall in the office dedicated to positive client feedback; she posted notes from clients praising the company's work, thanking the employees, or explaining how helpful they had been. You must constantly find ways to keep the company's mission front of mind and enable your people to keep their eyes on purpose.

Make Space for Purpose

In addition to consistently communicating purpose, one of the simplest ways to keep line of sight to purpose is to make space for it, providing dedicated times for team members to talk about the way their work makes a difference. Instead of just sharing your own stories, encourage employees to tell their colleagues, managers, and bosses how they have seen the real-life impact of their work. You are not only indirectly highlighting their efforts but also helping everyone in the room see how purpose comes to life.

Royal Bank of Canada, for example, has been our client for some time, and we have done a great deal of work in its retail bank operation. In the wake of the 2008–2009 financial crisis, when banks were being heavily criticized for their role in precipitating the Great Recession, we worked with RBC to discover the best way to communicate purpose to both employees and customers. Even though the large Canadian banks like RBC were not implicated in the cause of the recession in any meaningful way, the leaders felt it was important to help people see how RBC made a positive difference in the lives of its customers.

As part of our work with them, many RBC leaders implemented a simple practice we have taught for many years. The idea is to reserve time at the beginning of every meeting for people to share a story about how the bank made a real difference in the life of a customer or the community since last time the team met. As discussed, the leader can come prepared with examples of course, but the main goal is to get team members to identify their own stories. Over a six-month period, those branches where leaders followed this advice reported a significant, measurable increase in their team members' engagement.

Another way to make space for purpose is by providing opportunities for employees to communicate directly with the people they serve. It is one thing to speak to our people about the ideas behind our mission and purpose but quite another for them to see the direct impact that we're making together.

In chapter 6 we discuss the successful Molly Maid franchisee who framed the job purpose of his cleaning professionals as alleviating loneliness, especially with elderly customers. This franchisee regularly invites family members of his elderly clients, and often the clients themselves, to the franchise's staff meetings nearly every month. In real time employees get to hear how their presence in their customers' homes often represents one of the few meaningful social contacts for many elderly clients. Over time he told us that these visits made a real difference in raising the engagement and commitment of his team. They appreciated hearing directly from customers and saw how they were making a true difference in their lives.

When we worked with software company Advanced Management Systems (AMS), the division president for the federal government, Harry, would regularly bring in employees from the agencies that used the company's software. The clients talked about how AMS's products were helping agencies successfully carry out the work of the US government. Harry told us, "My people work hard to develop this software and implement it but rarely get to see what a difference it makes in real time for the people who use it." By connecting employees to clients, Harry gave his staff a direct line of sight to purpose.

Encouraging and facilitating this type of space to celebrate purpose draws employees in and engages them with their work and the organization's efforts. Dedicating time for group discussions or inviting clients to share their experiences enables your team to voice their thoughts and inspire one another while also receiving feedback from the primary purpose of the business—their customers. You are signaling that you care about all stakeholders involved, and you're taking an active role in connecting your team with their purpose.

EXERCISE *Connecting Recognition to Purpose*

One final way to create line of sight to purpose for employees is by connecting recognition to purpose. When we recognize team members for an accomplishment, they appreciate it, but they are also typically inspired to continue doing an outstanding job. Recognition should be direct and specific, showing how the person's actions exemplified the company's purpose. Whenever we praise someone verbally or in writing, we need to connect that appreciation to purpose. Consider the following.

- Instead of simply saying, "Thanks for doing a great job with that angry customer," try, "That customer was so frustrated, and you made a real difference for them by staying calm and letting them vent."

- Instead of simply saying, "Great job getting all those bags on board during that irregular operation yesterday," try, "Great job getting those bags on board yesterday. You made a lot of customers happy today, now that they have their bags. And they don't even know how hard you worked to do it—but I do!"

- Instead of "Thanks for being part of our recycling committee; you did a great job," try, "I heard great things about your work on the recycling committee. Thanks for doing your part to keep a great planet for my kids."

When you give direct, specific feedback, showing that you recognize how your employees' work has directly contributed to the company's overall purpose, you reward them for more than just a job well done. They understand how they can contribute to the company's mission and purpose most effectively and feel a sense of pride in knowing that they truly had an impact. Helping employees internalize that idea will produce even better results down the line. In the process you're closing the purpose gap and leading your people to ever-greater success.

CAN YOUR CUSTOMERS SEE YOUR PURPOSE?

In addition to employees, customers need to see line of sight to purpose. We must always be asking, *How do we make our impact real and visceral for our customers?* In so doing bear in mind that customers are skeptical about our claims toward purpose, and there is a great deal of cynicism about the goodness of companies. As discussed earlier, consumers are generally confused about whether the companies they buy from are good or simply trying to *seem* good. In other words, we have a real issue when it comes to stakeholders believing that we are sincere in our efforts.

Consumers are right to wonder if our focus on purpose is real and worthy of their loyalty. That's why it is necessary to connect with them authentically and show them how we're living our purpose—we cannot stress this concept enough. If we are unable to connect with our customers or exhibit that we truly care about their well-being, the causes that are important to them, and the state of society and the planet, the lessons in this book are all for naught.

Carol Cone, CEO of Carol Cone on Purpose, has been one of the leading voices in helping companies connect cause to customer for more than 20 years. Cone says that the formula to creating a line of sight to purpose for customers is simple but rarely followed:

"You need to get clear on what purposes in society you are best positioned to focus on. You need to be honest about your warts rather than pretend you are perfect. In the end, you want to find the human stories of who you are helping and make it real—telling those stories ideally in the words and voices of the real people you serve."

The purpose revolution requires a reorientation—a shift in the organization's consciousness—that asks the organization to adopt a mode of active listening and observation. We must seek to understand our customers' experiences and let our mission and actions come to the fore. Part of this movement involves showcasing your beliefs about the role of business in society so that customers know where you stand.

When commenting on his company's success on the global stage, Managing Director and Global CEO Subhanu Saxena said Cipla is now in the position to "show the world...that it is important for a business to have a purpose beyond profit; to have an eye for making a difference in the societies and the communities that it operates in."[2] Many times the ability to create this line of sight for your customers relies on new, innovative solutions to longstanding problems.

THE LEMONADE OF INSURANCE

The New York–based start-up Lemonade, for example, has taken a whole new approach to insurance. Though the tech entrepreneurs Daniel Schreiber and Shai Wininger had no background in the industry when they launched the company in September 2016, they saw a need for greater efficiency and the chance to make a real difference in people's lives.[3] The company uses state-of-the-art technology, including mobile compatibility and artificial intelligence, to move along the insurance process at lightning speed. Their model breaks from traditional insurance companies by taking a fixed fee out of customers' monthly payments (covering claims and other costs) and treating premiums as though they were essentially still their clients' money.[4] Any remaining money is returned through their annual "Giveback"—and here's where things get exciting.

Lemonade connects clients virtually to form groups of members who care about similar social causes. At the end of the year, the company implements the Giveback, donating any leftover money from the premiums collected throughout the year to the common causes the groups have identified. Here we see two things happening.

First, unlike traditional insurers, Lemonade does not rely on making money by keeping what it doesn't pay out in claims. This means it is willing to pay claims quickly, as it isn't losing out on any money. Second, social good is embedded in the actual business model, and customers are given an incredibly clear line of sight to purpose that is based on the values they have already identified as being important to them.

Visit the Lemonade website and right away you notice the clear, concise language used to explain the company's operations. It's accessible and easy to understand, not obfuscated by jargon and unnecessary complexity. The commitment to customers is front and center, followed by the commitment to doing good. Though Lemonade is still a small organization, its innovative approach connects customers with purpose, proving that in the purpose revolution disruption is likely to occur even in the most stagnant, longstanding industries.

EMERGING WAYS TO CLOSE THE CUSTOMER PERCEPTION GAP

One of the greatest challenges in the age of social good is closing the gap between customers' desire to support companies that are doing good and their skepticism about the reality behind the rhetoric. A new form of company has emerged that helps both well-intentioned companies and concerned consumers: the B Corporation. An independent nonprofit company, B Lab, administers an assessment that measures "the impact of a business on all of its stakeholders, including its workers, suppliers, community, and the environment. The assessment also captures best practices regarding mission, measurement, and governance [and]…the company's specific "Impact Business Models," which include the targeted, formal focus on benefiting a particular stakeholder through products and services or internal practices."[5]

As of this writing, more than 1,800 businesses in 32 countries and 60 industries with billions of dollars in assets have completed the B Impact Assessment to become certified B Corporations. Becoming a B Corp helps your company assess how you are doing with stakeholders while also providing customers and other businesses greater assurance that there is substance behind your purpose story. Along with the publisher of this book, Berrett-Koehler, other notable B-certified companies include New Belgium Brewing Company, Warby Parker, Seventh Generation, and MUD Jeans.

Benefit corporations are another new form of profit-based organizations emerging in response to the desire for purpose. Benefit corporations are "authorized by 33 US states and the District of Columbia [to have a] positive impact on society, workers, the community and the environment in addition to profit as its legally defined goals."[6]

Whereas with B Corp certification doing social good is voluntary, benefit corporations are legally bound to meet the following four requirements.

- **Public benefit.** The company must provide "general public benefit," which means "a material positive impact on society and the environment, i.e., maximum positive externalities and minimum negative."

- **Impacts on stakeholders.** Benefit corporation status makes it the fiduciary duty of the board of directors to "consider the impact of their decisions not only on shareholders but also on society and the environment."

- **Accountability.** Benefit corporations must assess their overall corporate, social, and environmental performance on a yearly basis using an independent third-party standard.

- **Transparency.** Benefit corporations must report their overall social and environmental performance to their shareholders and to the public in an annual benefit report.[7]

While the number of companies choosing this path is still relatively small, this new movement provides opportunities for profit-making organizations and entrepreneurs to hardwire aspirational purpose into their legal structure. Some more notable benefit corporations include Patagonia, Kickstarter, Plum Organics, King Arthur Flour, Solberg Manufacturing, Laureate Education, and AltSchool.

We see both of these emerging structures as a sign of where things are going and also as a way to close the purpose gap with customers.

Natura: Closing the Gap on Sustainability in Brazil

When our purpose is real and we live it, persistent effort at purpose can lead to public recognition. Founded in 1969, Natura is Brazil's largest cosmetics producer and the biggest cosmetics company in South America. Its central guiding principle is sustainability: "Everything our business has done has been based on a commitment of respect for the environment and social responsibility."[8] This focus is demonstrated across the whole supply chain, from raw materials sourced sustainability from the Brazilian rain forests, to logistics, manufacturing, packaging, and social responsibility.

For example, Natura has partnership agreements with 36 rural communities to provide traditional knowledge and sustainable ingredients; it provides incentives for local communities to preserve their natural resources. The company established a certification program of forest product providers to ensure that ingredients from the rain forests are sourced sustainably and in a socially responsible way. The Corporate Knights Order, announced each year at the World Economic Forum in Davos, ranked Natura the "second most committed business to sustainable development in the world."[9]

Such recognition by third parties such as Corporate Knights, B Lab, and the Dow Sustainability Index can help connect your customers with your brand and purpose. When customers see the benefits they receive as well as those you provide to others, they will want to join you wholeheartedly—and investors won't be far behind.

JUST SAY SO

One of the simplest ways to create line of sight is to be as clear as you can on your packaging or at the point of sale about who you are and what you stand for. The Unilever study of global consumers referenced earlier showed that the easier we can make it for customers to see our purpose, the more likely they are to act on their desire to buy good.

On a recent speaking tour in Zurich, John visited a small local restaurant chain called "B. Good." We all want good food, and we want to buy food we feel good about. But what does that really mean? On a large wall in the restaurant was a sign that took up half the wall, and it looked like chalkboard. At the top were the simple words *What we mean by Good!* Underneath were four simple things with brief details to back it up: *we buy from local farmers and families, we have real people make the food, we respect the seasons,* and *we make our communities a little better.* On one sign, right where you could see it, were the four reasons B. Good was more than a name.

Make it real, make it clear, make it easy to see, and live up to it. That is called *line of sight.*

LINE OF SIGHT FOR INVESTORS

Line of sight to purpose is critical for employees and important for customers, so we'd be remiss not to mention investors as well. Though we emphasize employees and customers in this book, investors and their potential influence cannot be understated. Many investors today believe that there is better value in sustainably run companies. The majority of institutional investors surveyed by MIT Sloan said that improved revenue performance from sustainability is a strong reason to invest.[10] The findings show that more than 80 percent of investors believe that sustainability performance drives long-term value creation in a company.

The US SIF Foundation reported that a 2015 Calvert Investments survey found that once individual investors were educated about sustainable-investing opportunities, they expressed interest.[11] The survey found that 87 percent of respondents want investments aligned with their values. That said, a major problem exists regarding creating a line of sight to purpose for investors.

The demand for sustainability reporting is on the rise, but communication about such efforts to investors is not. A 2014 Nasdaq Advisory Services study of 500 publicly traded companies found that only about one-fifth of US companies communicate sustainability information in their reporting.[12] In Europe the figure was just over 50 percent. Within organizations, a 2015 *MIT Sloan Management Review* and National Investor Relations Institute study found that only 24 percent of investor relations professionals are asked by leadership to inform investors about the impact of sustainability on their bottom line.[13] The report also found that around 40 percent are given no direction whatsoever on sustainability reporting, while another 80 percent never include sustainability talking points in investor communications.

Like they do with employees and customers, companies must clearly communicate their purpose to investors and show how that purpose leads to excellent results. A great opportunity to draw a line of sight for investors is in a company's annual shareholder letter. Don't just post your numbers—back them up by explaining how your purpose-driven approach has led to this success throughout the year. Include data on how many employees took advantage of volunteer opportunities. Show investors how consumers and customers engaged with the brand through social media around sustainability or charitable efforts. And don't forget to get personal and convey compelling true stories about the impact on real individuals of your efforts toward a better, more sustainable world.

Another option is to prepare CSR reports and make them available online for investors to review. CSR reports must be clear and engaging; they provide detailed information about a company's sustainability efforts and are quickly becoming standard for the most forward-thinking organizations. A 2015 investment study by Ernst & Young found that 59 percent of investors consider CSR reports to be essential or important to investment decisions, with nearly 62 percent indicating that nonfinancial data is relevant to all industrial sectors today.[14] For larger companies, data on such topics as a decrease in your company's greenhouse gas emissions or how you've addressed a socioeconomic problem in a developing nation are typically included.

No matter how you decide to create a line of sight to purpose for investors or potential investors, you need to ensure that it is not only clear and consistent but also authoritative. Some investors may still be wary of "purpose" as a deciding factor in where to commit their money, so show them the true benefits of a purpose-driven culture and how it results in higher earnings and a better world.

EXERCISE   *How to Create a Clear Line of Sight to Purpose*

Have a meeting with other leaders or your team to explore what you are doing now and what you could be doing to create a clear line of sight to purpose. Use chart paper or a whiteboard to draw the following table. Have participants write down their ideas on sticky notes and post them to each quadrant. Have an open discussion about what to keep doing, what to start doing, and how to communicate and engage others.

Action Questions	As Leaders	As an Organization
What are we doing now?		
What could we be doing?		

THE FIRST QUESTION YOU ASK MATTERS

When it comes to keeping line of sight for employees, customers, and investors, one of the most powerful messages we send as leaders relates to the questions we ask. Inge Thulin, the CEO of 3M, talked to us about the need for leaders to be aware of the first thing they ask about when they visit different parts of the company. In the case of 3M, Thulin believes that sustainability is at the very core of his company's reason for being, as well as his own personal purpose: "When I visit different plants or parts of our company, I try hard to make sure that the first question I ask is what they are doing about sustainability." By making that the first or among the first questions he asks, his message is clear: doing good is job #1.

This concept is as true for those running a team or a small business as it is for a $31 billion company. If I am the head of a bank branch, my first question shouldn't be "How many mortgages did we sell today?" It should be "Did we help anyone buy their dream home today?" If I run a shoe store, my first question shouldn't be "How are sales looking this month?" It should be "Did we make someone's day and help them find happiness today?" We need to train ourselves to remember that every question we ask, story we tell, and action we recognize sends a message about what really matters to us. It either focuses line of sight to purpose or to something else. The choice is ours.

Shoes and Happiness

Town Shoes Limited is a premier retailer in Canada and a division of DSW, one of the largest shoe retailers in the world. Early on, TSL's president, Simon Nankervis, hadn't given a lot of thought to the role that purpose might play in business. As Town Shoes went through a difficult period, however, he realized the role that purpose played in his own personal journey. He saw his personal purpose as *to live morally and inspire my family and teams to achieve the greatness within them,* but he wasn't sure if he saw a similar sense of purpose in the company. He needed to help his team connect to something greater.

"Prior to beginning this work," Nankervis told us, "I had never given our purpose any deliberate thought. Rather I acted out of a sense of the personal journey I was undertaking. Not surprisingly, as we commenced this journey it caused me to evaluate my purpose and ultimately recognize that I had been loving my life through my purpose." The process he followed to engage his team is instructive and shows the importance of drawing a line of sight to purpose.

First, he convened the executive leadership team and explained why he believed that purpose was critical to the life and the future of the organization: "I discussed with them the difference between purpose and vision/mission statements. We then spent time discussing what would Canada be like without Town Shoes, and why do we matter?" Each leader was asked to make their own purpose board—a visual representation of the people, places, and things that define their individual purpose.

"We didn't try to craft a statement," Nankervis said, "but rather we just wrote down all the things that each executive felt or thought about TSL. Initially, everyone expressed their observations or thoughts, but as we continued to delve into what it is about TSL that's special or unique, we finally got to an emotional place. We got to a series of words that really defined the emotional connection all of us had to our brand."

The purpose that emerged was simple but powerful: *happiness through self-expression*. This was the leaders' reasoning: Shoes for most people are a form of self-expression, and when someone can express their true self, they feel happy. The purpose also felt all-encompassing. Happiness could come from employees working in a place where they could be themselves and grow as people and as professionals. The purpose could also integrate outside societal issues or problems that are important to staff members. For example, the company has taken efforts to help reduce violence against women; in doing so, happiness is increased for everyone who is affected, including children. This is a great example of a purpose that works for customers, employees, and society.

The leaders presented their initial purpose statement to a broader group and asked for their thoughts. Amazingly, the purpose resonated with everyone for vastly different reasons, but it gave the team a clear sense of why they do what they do, not just the business they are in. Nankervis says, "Defining purpose almost seemed cathartic because our team had struggled to understand the reason TSL was unique and special. It felt like naming our purpose was akin to allowing someone who had been holding their breath an opportunity to breathe again—you could feel the collective sigh."

TSL's retail outlets started connecting to the purpose right away. Says Nankervis, "Each of the teams that has embraced our purpose has found a new sense of pride in the work they do. They understand what the company expects of them, and they have begun to celebrate delivering on our purpose." The stores also started using social media to amplify their purpose (line of sight). "Almost immediately, we saw the teams adopting our new hashtag #happinesthroughselfexpression. We continue to see the teams proudly adopt the hashtag whenever they do anything that reflects our purpose."

Stories of how TSL's teams were changing customers' lives through purpose quickly began emerging. At one store a woman with a transgender child was so touched by how they were treated with care, dignity, and understanding that the mother wrote a letter of commendation for the sales associate. At another location a middle-aged man who suffered from diabetes and had lost two toes told one of the associates about his disability. He worried that she may not be comfortable assisting him, but she responded by saying that she was honored to help fit him. He was so gracious; he also delivered a letter of commendation for the associate. Sharing these stories with other associates and the public truly helps draw a line of sight to purpose, demonstrating how Town Shoes is making a real difference for people every day.

When asked why purpose matters, Nankervis simply says: "Purpose is pivotal to an organization's reason for being. It is the lifeblood of a team and gives an organization direction. Purpose has enabled me to rally our entire team. Both our associates and customers benefit from an organization driven by purpose because it ties together not only the in-store experience but also the way our associates approach the daily tasks."

BEST PRACTICES FOR
CREATING A LINE OF SIGHT TO PURPOSE

- Make space for purpose. Dedicate time for team members to talk about the way their work makes a difference.

- Bring together customers, community members, or consumers to discuss how your products or services make a difference in their lives.

- Have purpose updates twice annually. Do a roadshow (a traveling presentation) of CSR efforts and results and bring it to life with multimedia—videos of programs in action, employees volunteering, and similar efforts—not just facts and figures. Do this even if you are a frontline leader so that everyone feels connected to the organization's purpose.

- Begin meetings, presentations, and formal written communications by emphasizing the company's mission and purpose with stories about how your products or services are making a real difference in the lives of your stakeholders.

- Insist that even when difficult decisions must be made, the choices are based on the company purpose first, not just the shareholders' interests.

- Don't tell just your own stories about the impact the company is having on customers; dedicate time for your team members and employees to share their stories with colleagues and leaders, as well.

- Give your team members direct, specific feedback, showing that you recognize how their work has directly contributed to the company's purpose.

- Hold your own version of a "lineup meeting" to ensure that your team is on board with purpose every day.

- Join the 20 percent of US companies that communicate sustainability information in their reporting, supplying stats on your efforts and actual results in annual shareholder letters and other corporate communications.

CHAPTER 9

How to Win Talent in the Purpose Revolution

W HILE INTERVIEWING LEADERS ACROSS INDUSTRIES FOR THIS book, we found many recurring themes when discussing the purpose revolution and how companies and talent are seeing a new trend emerge. A story we often heard in a variety of forms revolved around not just connecting purpose with current employees but attracting new employees through purpose, as well.

Take, for example, a story told us by Kiersten Robinson, executive director of human resources, global markets, at Ford Motor Company. Robinson did a stint in HR for Ford in China. Her responsibilities included leading new-employee orientation: "As part of the program, I would routinely ask new employees in China the top three reasons why they decided to work for Ford. Inevitably, a large majority would have our company's vision to create a better world in that top three." Ford's clear, concise purpose, stated loudly and boldly, had resonated throughout the world with top talent.

We heard a similar story from Joey Bergstein, the CEO of Seventh Generation. Bergstein knows firsthand the power of an authentic purpose to attract and retain the best talent. One of his top scientists, who had invented Fantastic and Formula 409 at Clorox, joined the Seventh Generation team because of the impact he knew he could make there, believing in its purpose and values. Bergstein's head of

R&D, who had had a great career at P&G and Church & Dwight, also wanted to do something more meaningful with his career, so he chose to work at Seventh Generation. "We blow others out of the water when it comes to attracting talent in our sector, and other companies try to lure our talent from the company," he told us.

According to the *2017 Deloitte Global Human Capital Trends* report, there are widespread "talent and skill shortages," making attracting the best talent "a top concern of business leaders," with 83 percent of executives saying that talent acquisition is "important or very important." The report found that "employees are demanding new careers and career models," with one key driver being a job that provides an enriching, meaningful experience along with opportunities to learn, grow, and contribute.[1] People are thinking differently about the meaning of work over the course of their lives. As the purpose revolution continues, we see the career-ladder model being discarded in favor of the new life-journey model that is emerging.

Purpose attracts top talent from all generations. Research found that 85 percent of US employees said they "were likely to stay longer with an employer that showed a high level of social responsibility," whereas researchers in the United Kingdom found that 42 percent of employees *globally* say it matters to them to work for a company that is making a positive difference in society; 44 percent thought meaningful work that helped others was more important than a high salary; and 53 percent would work harder if their company benefited society or was making a difference to others.[2] The number jumps to six in 10 for millennials, who said "a 'sense of purpose' is part of the reason they chose to work for their company."[3]

According to Gallup, a full 50 percent of millennials say they'd rather take a pay cut than work for a company with unethical business practices.[4] Deloitte's *2015 Millennial Survey* also found an "impact gap" among millennials, who said business meets expectations on job creation but is "underperforming on social advancement, helping employees, etc."[5] This is a huge disconnect.

With a talent and skill shortage and a cultural shift from the "old ways" of work, companies are competing over employees more vigorously than ever before. In this time of talent grab, you need to ask, *What makes our organization or team stand out above the others?* We have found that meaningful work is fast becoming the magnet for attracting top talent to an organization. Authentic purpose-driven companies offer this type of work, along with opportunities to grow and make a difference in the world. Recruiting the best talent is all about helping them discover their life's journey and acting as their partner along the way. Just as with your current employees, customers, and investors, you must connect your potential employees' purpose to your company's mission and purpose, as well.

BUILD PURPOSE INTO RECRUITING AND ONBOARDING

Recruiting top talent starts with giving candidates a compelling mission and purpose that motivates them to work for you—not a description of *what* they will do but an inspiring image of *how* they will find meaning and help you change the world. For example, at Airbnb you have the chance to *create a world that inspires human connection.* Dell Computer Company invites job seekers to contribute *time, technology, and know-how to make the world a better place.* Chemistry, a tech-powered, global business consultancy, promises to *give everyone the opportunity to be brilliant at work.* Expedia states on its website, "Here's what we look for when we're interviewing: passionate travelers who want to make a tangible difference."

To be heard in the crowded world of recruiting, your call needs to be to a higher purpose—something that says that by working for your company, employees will find personal meaning and opportunities to grow and contribute to something bigger than themselves. Of course, these types of commitments must be upheld and supported or you'll quickly find that top talent is passing you by. We regularly suggest four ways that any company or leader, small or large, can build purpose and meaning into the hiring process to attract the best and brightest.

Showcase Purpose Up Front

The interview process is one of the most effective means to demonstrate to candidates and potential employees that purpose is front and center in your company. On applications and during interviews, clearly feature your values and purpose. Make sure that the job descriptions you post online, whether on your own website or through a third-party source, speak directly to the people you're trying to attract in today's evolving market. Don't just include the duties, requirements, and responsibilities of the position; describe your company's story, its ethos, and how its purpose ties to your team members' values and goals. Be bold and highlight how your purpose is integral to every aspect of the company and culture. Recruits want to see what your company is truly made of, and if you're able to generate interest in your purpose, they'll be willing to go above and beyond in the interview process.

Acumen, the global nonprofit investment fund, states its purpose in its "manifesto," which says in part, "It thrives on moral imagination: the humility to see the world as it is, and the audacity to imagine the world as it could be.... It's the radical idea of creating hope in a cynical world. Changing the way the world tackles poverty and building a world based on dignity."[6]

Acumen has designed a recruitment process that enables it to identify potential employees who share the organization's purpose. Instead of simply asking interested candidates to submit a résumé and cover letter, the HR department also has candidates respond to a series of short essay questions that relate to the position. For instance, one question they may include is "How would you describe your interest in 'impact investing' versus regular private equity or venture capital investing?" Not only does the answer give Acumen's recruiter insight into the candidate but the candidate sees that Acumen is dedicated to its mission by asking this question in the first place.

Remember that this may be the first interaction some of the best emerging talent has with your company, so think creatively when it comes to recruiting and interviewing. Emzingo, mentioned in chapter 7, designed a unique interview process for a purpose-driven IT consulting company, involving teams of potential recruits performing a real-life consulting session with a socially conscious enterprise. The company can not only evaluate candidates' work in real time but also send the powerful message that *here is the kind of good you are going to get to do if you come work with us.* Think of creative ways to connect potential candidates to your purpose and expose them to your good work before they even get the job.

Make Your Mission Real for Hires

After featuring your purpose front and center, provide candidates with compelling evidence of how your company lives its mission. Like consumers, recruits are skeptical of company claims to be purpose driven and sustainable; they want concrete proof. You must anticipate this skepticism and be prepared with evidence. Show candidates how they will personally be involved in the good work that you're doing. Demonstrating with specific data how company initiatives have made an impact in the lives of others is excellent, but you'll also want to approach recruits in a more personal manner.

You may want to connect potential recruits with a current employee who's working on the same team that they'd be joining. That may feel like standard fare, but the twist is to ensure that the current team member focuses on purpose and the real impact your team makes. Ask team members to share with potential recruits how they have connected to the organization's purpose and what gives them meaning working for you. Even better is if you also put them in touch with someone who works in an entirely different department whose role is unrelated to the prospective employee's.

As discussed throughout the book, the company's purpose and mission must be owned and embraced by everyone throughout the organization. If your company has successfully reached this goal, anyone, at any level, should be able to talk to a candidate about the mission and values that permeate the culture, showing that you are serious when it comes to purpose. Bringing in current employees in real time to talk about what working for a purposeful company has meant to them shows that your company's authenticity is real and tangible.

During the interview ask prospects what their life purpose is and what they want to contribute. Ask about times when they have lived their deepest values at work and what issues they care most about. If you are interviewing people who will work on your team, share your personal purpose. Focusing on these questions and your values during interviews sends the message that purpose is important to your organization; it also increases the likelihood of hiring people with a purpose orientation toward work. Don't be shy to ask about purpose—you want to signal that it is central to your team's work.

Show You Care about Employees' Values

The values of purpose-driven organizations are the foundation of their culture, but concepts like sustainability and social responsibility cannot flourish if the company's basic values have yet to be lived. It's necessary to show candidates that, in addition to customers and your core purpose, you truly care about your employees' well-being. When you treat your employees with respect and gratitude, you demonstrate that the company is serious about helping its people grow and succeed. This type of environment fosters a workforce that feels supported and can therefore concentrate on the mission at hand. Candidates understand that if you are treating your people right, you are likely doing right by your customers and society as well.

Zapier is a Silicon Valley start-up that offers a platform for connecting apps to automate tasks. It recently offered a $10,000 "de-location package" for employees willing to relocate away from

Silicon Valley. The reason? To support employees who want to improve their family's standard of living by moving to areas with lower housing costs. CEO Wade Foster told *The Guardian,* "A lot of folks just have a difficult time making the Bay Area a long-term home."[7] Providing flexible work alternatives is another way to show that you care about employees. Zapier embraces a work-from-home model to enrich employees' lifestyles and family lives. All of its employees work remotely because, as Foster said, "We've seen the technology advance to a state where people can legitimately work anywhere in the world."

Think about ways that your company helps make your employees' lives better and be ready to talk about them with potential employees. What initiatives has your company implemented in recent years due to technology or changing demographics that show how you support your teams? Whether you provide flexible hours, the opportunity to work remotely, or compensation for relocation, consider what actions you can highlight to share with candidates and then tie them back to the company's mission.

Make Your Career Site a Purpose Site

Every organization should have an interactive career website as a testimonial to its purpose-driven culture. Career websites should be highly engaging and easy to navigate while effectively providing job seekers with a genuine *feel* for the organization and what it stands for. Ask yourself: *Does my company's employment website engage prospective talent? Does it show meaningful, purposeful work in action? Does it provide clear and compelling statements about our values and what we stand for? Does it show opportunities to learn, grow, contribute, and make the world a better place? Does it provide a behind-the-scenes look into what it's like to work here?* Do you feature the *voice of the employee* so that job seekers can see and hear from people like themselves how great your company is to work for? If you can't answer yes to most of these questions, it's time to consider updating the site.

Put Purpose at Center Stage

Airbnb, which won Glassdoor's Best Place to Work in 2016, part of Glassdoor's annual Employees' Choice Awards, features one of the best career websites we have ever seen. When you visit the careers section of the Airbnb website, the company purpose, *Create a world that inspires human connection,* tops the page.[8] Note that there is no mention about hotel alternatives, short-term lodging, or vacation rentals. Instead they highlight the connection of the team and the company's goal to start a movement: "No global movement springs from individuals. It takes an entire team united behind something big."

The website refers to caring for others, building with the long term in mind, participating in the community and culture, and demonstrating an ability to grow. It appeals to what matters to the purpose-driven workforce by showing what they can be and do at Airbnb. The company summarizes these ideas through a simple credo: *Create. Learn. Play.*

Photos and videos on the site show employees in an open, warm, and unconventional organizational setting, with couches, colorful décor, and a variety of work spaces. Included is a section of YouTube videos featuring employees talking about why they like working for Airbnb. They mention such aspects as a sense of community, feeling at home and like they belong, and knowing that the work their team does really touches the lives of their guests, fulfilling the company's mission and purpose. Other videos show colleagues interacting, as well as testimonials from interns and employees describing opportunities to contribute, grow, and experience a sense of family at Airbnb.

Airbnb also gives prospective recruits a behind-the-scenes look at meaningful work in action. Another website video showcases the development of the Airbnb iPhone app and features the actual engineers who worked on the project. The employees narrate and walk the viewer through the process of developing the app. It shows smart, highly engaged people working together for a meaningful cause. The video gives job seekers an inside look at Airbnb's open-space format, teamwork, creative process, and employee enthusiasm as the engineers design groundbreaking technology for their customers.

EXERCISE   *Revamping the Career Website*

If you're having trouble recruiting top talent, it might be time to see how your career website can be reworked to attract more traffic and engage prospective employees. Compare it with the Airbnb site and note the similarities and differences. Also you check out Dell's site, which employs a similar approach.[9] Dell's global talent brand and tools team revolutionized its employee website to provide clear and consistent brand messages and interactive features. In addition to employee profiles, the site includes videos, images, and links for graduate and undergraduate opportunities to reach a broad audience of job seekers. Dell also posts videos to YouTube and other sites to reach potential candidates.

After looking over both sites, consider how your site measures up. If you feel you might be missing something, call a meeting to discuss the site and brainstorm ideas for improving it. Here are some points to cover:

- Your company's purpose statement front and center

- Testimonials or blog posts from current or past employees about their work experience

- Videos of interview team members discussing how they interpret the company's purpose and bring it to life through their work

- Job descriptions that highlight the company's values and goals, especially those that connect with purpose over profit

- Any type of interactive features that will grab the candidates' attention and motivate them to explore the site completely

---

MAKE EMPLOYEES
PURPOSE AMBASSADORS

Whether showcasing your purpose, proving that your mission is authentic, providing evidence of how you care about your employees, or designing an engaging website, your goal is to generate top talent's interest. We have found that one of the most effective ways to accomplish this objective is with your employees' support. Just like employees are your best brand ambassadors for customers, they are also your greatest talent brand ambassadors.

But what is your *talent brand*? What stories, experiences, and images are associated with working for your company? How do job candidates see the company making a difference in the world? How do employees find meaning and purpose working for you? The most believable ambassadors for your company are the people who already work there. After top talent read up on your organization and check your website to see what your company is all about, they will look to social media and their social networks to learn what it means to work for you—in fact, they may even start there.

Film candid videos—like those featured on your career website— of current team members talking about what the company's purpose means to them and how they contribute to that purpose in their work. Post these videos on YouTube, Facebook, and other social media sites, especially in conjunction with job posts to increase your reach. The *2017 Deloitte Global Human Capital Trends* report points out that, according to PeopleScout, "Job postings on Facebook that feature videos receive 36 percent more applications."[10]

Expedia UK, which received Glassdoor's Best Place to Work in 2017, features several employee videos on social media describing how the company's purpose, culture, and values are important to them. One employee says, "Travel as a force for good in the world inspires people at Expedia. We have a great culture, but it all begins with purpose. We believe travel helps make the world smaller and it enriches people's experiences…but that travel also has an impact on society. As Mark Twain once wrote, 'Travel is fatal to prejudice, bigotry, and narrow-mindedness,' and if we can also contribute to that, then we're extremely proud."[11]

Encourage employees to "share the good" through social media—and make it easy for them to do that. Stories directly from employees who experience purpose at work are an incredible magnet for attracting new talent. Provide your employees with links, pictures, and information about events they were part of or the result of projects they worked on. This material could be regarding a community outreach or volunteer program or more directly linked to how the company's products and services are helping others. Also supply employees with stories and examples of the good *you* are doing that they will be excited to share with people in their networks. Encourage employees to post such information on YouTube or other social media sites through first-person testimonials.

Of course, not every aspect of employees' efforts as talent brand ambassadors needs to be online, nor should it be. You should help employees expand their networks and influence a larger pool of potential candidates. Reid Hoffman, cofounder and former executive chairman of LinkedIn, encourages organizations to extend beyond the company's boundaries by "subsidizing the building of employee networks outside of the organization."[12]

As your best ambassadors, employees increase your reach through strong employee networks, so it makes sense to encourage and pay for employees to attend conferences, present papers, sit on committees and boards, and have a strong presence in the broader landscape. When they're out there in person, showing their support of your company's efforts, employees from other organizations take notice. The more your people are involved, the more awareness they raise about the company and the company's mission and purpose.

Another way to support and maintain an employee network is to establish an alumni group to keep in touch with past employees. Sponsor events to function as reunions to bring people together and maintain their sense of family and history with your company. Build a lifetime relationship with your talent, as you never know where they'll end up and whom they'll connect with and influence. Your employee network therefore serves as a recruiting tool, especially if not just current but also past employees are singing your company's praises and spreading the message that you're serious about purpose.

As talent brand ambassadors, your employees play a critical role in your company's future. Through mutual support, both the organization's and the individuals' long-term goals can be met and even surpassed. By helping employees help you attract the best and brightest talent, a cooperative relationship is formed, benefiting everyone involved. Your current employees are also in tune with what potential employees want out of their jobs. I'm sure you've guessed it by now: It's not just financial reward. It's passion, meaningful work, and the opportunity for growth and contributing to the greater good.

EXERCISE *Are Your Job Postings Fit for Purpose?*

Look at the current job openings posted on your company's website or any job you are about to post for your organization. Pick a post that is particularly interesting and take some time to dissect it.

- What is the most effective part of the post?

- Does it clearly state what value the job adds? What is meaningful about this job?

- Does the post speak to the type of top talent you're pursuing by engaging them beyond the duties of the position? If so, highlight those phrases or sections that seem most compelling and consider how they connect with your company's stated mission, values, and purpose.

- Are they generic or are they on target and specific to your brand? If you were a prospective candidate, how would you respond?

If you find that the posts on your site do not go beyond the most basic description of responsibilities, describe in writing your experience at your job and how it connects to the overall purpose the company espouses.

- Think about how the importance behind what you do every day and what the organization does collectively can be positioned more prominently.

- Think of the job purpose over the job function. This not only helps you reconsider how you're currently approaching potential employees but should also remind you of what brought you to the company in the first place. It's always good to recall your personal purpose and see how your company has lived up to your expectations. Your employees will regularly do the same.

3M Magnet for Talent

For a good example of how purpose can become a talent magnet, take a closer look at 3M, which has more than 90,000 team members around the world. The company has grown from a small mining operation founded in Minnesota in 1902 to become one of the most diversified science-based manufacturing companies in the world. Its original name was the Minnesota Mining and Manufacturing Company, which long ago was shortened to 3M. It has always been characterized by a certain Midwestern humility. You won't see 3M bragging very much, but its sense of purpose is palpable, as the company is tackling some of the world's biggest challenges. One thing it isn't shy to talk about is how working to create a sustainable present and future has become its rallying cry.

Caring about the environment has been a way of life for 3M, dating as far back as 1975, when it introduced the Pollution Prevention Pays (3P) program. Although the idea had been around for some time, the company made it central to the enterprise. 3P seeks to eliminate pollution at the source through product reformulation, process modification, equipment redesign, and recycling and reuse of waste materials. Over the ensuing years, 3M prevented billions of pounds of pollutants from entering the ecosystem while saving billions of dollars both internally and for the businesses it serves.

3M has an inspiring, clearly articulated, purpose: *3M technology advancing every company, 3M products enhancing every home, and 3M innovation improving every life.* We think it is among the best examples of a company's purpose being an almost perfect fit both to its core business and to thriving in the age of social good. While that purpose is advanced in thousands of products that help businesses, homes, and individuals get things done, the company has increasingly focused on environmental sustainability as a key part of its purpose.

When Inge Thulin became the CEO in 2012, he called more than 40 other CEOs, present and former, to ask them what they would have done differently and what advice they would give him. His takeaway was to have a clear vision right from the start. He began working on that vision while he was the chief operating officer and introduced it his second day in office. Sustainability was a key part of that vision.

A focus on taking care of nature was deeply embedded in Thulin from his upbringing in Sweden, where being outdoors is part of the national identity. Sustainability seemed a natural focus because it was an issue 3M clients were struggling with; it was also a cause that the company could tackle internally while also helping every business, home, and person find solutions. "Many people saw the sustainability challenge as a threat, but to us it was an opportunity."

Thulin is unequivocal about both the role of senior leaders in driving purpose and the importance of embedding sustainability into everything we do as leaders: "Every time I am doing a presentation, I try to talk about sustainability, try to make it the first question I ask people. We ask every division to have clear goals around sustainability, and I do everything I can to reinforce the purpose." He admits that the company has a long way to go but is proud of the progress they have made thus far. 3M has made great strides toward reducing energy use and waste while setting ambitious targets to help its clients reduce greenhouse gas emissions by 250 million tons.

The exciting thing is that people are noticing—especially the young talent 3M will need to fulfill its grand ambition of improving every life. In its 2017 annual report, the company noted that in a survey by the National Institute of High School Scholars, 3M was ranked as the top place to work for millennials. Not at all surprising, in the purpose revolution the best talent want more than a paycheck, and improving every life and helping solve some of the world's biggest problems sounds like a pretty good reason to get up in the morning.

BEST PRACTICES FOR RECRUITING PURPOSE-DRIVEN TALENT

- In your company's job descriptions and on the career page of your website, show candidates your compelling mission and purpose to motivate them to want to work for you. Do not focus the job description on *what they will do* but rather *how they will find meaning* and help you change the world.

- On applications and during interviews, feature your company's values and purpose so that candidates see them front and center and immediately understand the role they play in your organization.

- When developing job descriptions, describe the company's story, what's important to you, and how your company's purpose ties to your employees' own values and goals.

- In the interview process, whether written or verbal, ask candidates questions that signal what matters most to the company in terms of purpose.

- Connect job candidates with current employees—both those in the candidate's potential team as well as in other departments—to show how the company's purpose permeates the entire culture and is not just specific to one division or team.

- Explain any flexible work alternatives so that candidates can see how your company supports your workers through enriching their lifestyles and standards of living. Help them understand how this indirectly or directly connects to your company's purpose.

- Feature testimonials from your employees, interns, and customers on the company's career website and via social media, describing their experiences and how your company's work makes a difference to them personally and to the world.

- Post candid videos to social media of current team members talking about what the company's purpose means to them and how they get to contribute to that purpose in their work.

- Encourage employees to share on social media the good that your company is doing, and make it easy for them by providing them with content related to events they took part in or the results of their work.

- Establish company alumni groups to keep in touch with past employees to maintain them as your talent brand ambassadors.

CHAPTER 10

Eight Practices for Thriving in the Age of Social Good

07=18=18

THROUGHOUT THIS BOOK WE HAVE TALKED ABOUT THE PURPOSE revolution and what those winning in the revolution are doing to enable engagement and competitive advantage. We have provided prescriptive steps and advice on how to thrive in this age of social good, where to get started, and how to succeed over the long term, but you won't reap the rewards without sincere effort, consistency, and, most of all, *discipline,* which we define as hardwired practices that forge a path of least resistance to change.

For example, many weight-loss programs start with house-cleaning—getting rid of all the junk food in your home and stocking only the good stuff. That way, when you reach for the midnight snack, all you have are healthy choices. By eating that healthy snack, as opposed to hopping in your car and driving to a fast-food joint, you exhibit a sense of discipline. You also show discipline when you go to the gym or pool at the same time every day, even if you're tired. You will succeed because you've hardwired the practice and performed it even when you weren't in the mood.

In this chapter we want to leave you with practical ways to drive a purpose culture every single day. Just like everything else worth striving for—careers, relationships, happiness, love—this goal takes discipline and a relentless pursuit of something greater than ourselves. It requires the discipline of key practices done often. Some of these actions are large and some are small, but they all contribute to the mission of a purpose-driven company, involving employees, customers, community, and investors—all the stakeholders that we affect directly and indirectly.

The Ritz-Carlton teaches us important lessons about the power of simple disciplines and ongoing efforts to drive a purpose culture. Diana Oreck, former vice president of the Ritz-Carlton Leadership Center, is quoted on the Ritz-Carlton Leadership Center website: "Your culture must be enlivened every day. It's not enough to talk about your organizational culture when your P&L has gone south."[1] One thing the Ritz-Carlton does to "enliven" this each day is to keep its purpose on the front burner. For example, the company provides every employee with a credo card so the credo and employee promise are always at their fingertips. In every Ritz-Carlton, the Carlton motto, credo, and employee promise are posted publicly. These reminders make what's most important highly visible. They focus on what is valued, guide interactions with guests, and provide clear decision-making advice: always err on the side of the purpose no matter what.

And everyone is clear about purpose: "The Ladies and Gentlemen—the employees of the Ritz-Carlton—understand that their highest mission is the 'genuine care and comfort of our guests.'" As noted on the Carlton Leadership Center website, "their job function may be bellman, server or housekeeper, but their purpose is to provide legendary service. Having a common purpose unifies your team and strengthens your culture."[2]

PRACTICE 1:
EVERY LEADER IS A PURPOSE PROMOTER

A key lever for driving a purpose culture is to have leadership model the way. As a leader you must share your personal higher purpose on a regular basis. Talk about your life as a leader, the choices you have made, and what you stand for. During all-hands meetings, have senior team members or the business owner discuss their personal sense of purpose, as well as how that plays out in their role at the company. Ask them to describe the organization's higher purpose, how they make decisions with purpose in mind, and how they see the company making the world a better place. Modeling the way demonstrates real commitment and makes exploring and talking about purpose a normative part of the organizational culture. It also inspires others to think more deeply about their purpose and contributions.

Connect your team's everyday duties to the bigger picture of the organization's mission and purpose. You can inspire people by regularly referring to how their work makes a difference. One senior leader at a global pharmaceutical company based in France explained to us, "Sometimes our day-to-day work in the development phase is so removed from the commercial product that it is easy to lose sight of how important our contribution is. I make it a point to connect our team's work to the bigger picture, how we contribute to new therapeutic discoveries, and the difference it makes in the lives of the patients who use them."

Mark Southern, who heads the airports division for Air Canada, likes to remind his leaders and team members that a great many tears are shed at airports: "I like to remind them that for the people who travel on our flights, it can be an emotional experience, and it's my job to show the team that they can make a difference, turning those tears into positive experiences." Southern often speaks about his own personal purpose in a way that reminds every team member how serving others with *class and care* (Air Canada's mantra) is more than just a business strategy.

PRACTICE 2:
EVERY DECISION IS A PURPOSE DECISION

Remember that every decision is a purpose decision. You must take a stand for what you believe in and never leave it out of the decision equation. This approach has been paying off for Unilever. In 2014

CEO Paul Polman wrote in an article for the *McKinsey Quarterly*, "Thinking in the long term has removed enormous shackles from our organization. I really believe that's part of the strong success we've seen over the past five years. Better decisions are being made....We have moved to a more mature dialogue with our investor base about what strategic actions serve Unilever's best interests in the long term versus explaining short-term movements."[3]

When driving change initiatives, promote them based on values, not just business imperatives. Help others see the deeper purpose behind a strategy to find common ground. By so doing you stimulate engagement, as everyone owns some piece of the bigger purpose or promise. For example, TELUS CEO Darren Entwistle told us, "Our brand promise is the future is friendly." Working with the organization, he keeps that brand promise up front: "So, my retort to people is, 'So what the heck are you doing about it?' Are you really answering that question? The driving force for us now is how are we making and answering that question."

Keeping purpose at the center in the decision equation disciplines people to always ask, *How are we, and how am I, contributing to the common good that our company hopes to deliver?* No matter what size your company or team, when we as leaders connect every change to our reason for being, that is when magic happens.

You need to tie mission and purpose goals to incentives. In our conversation with Seventh Generation CEO Joey Bergstein, he told us that an "important element of our incentive system is that everyone gets an annual bonus at every level, and a portion of that incentive is based on delivering on our Corporate Consciousness Goals, so the incentive includes the mission focus."

What you pay attention to grows. Making mission goals part of the incentive program not only focuses attention on what matters most but also motivates people to dedicate time, energy, and resources to make these happen. It also stimulates innovation and new ideas as teams search for ways to deliver on the mission. Bergstein emphasizes aligning financial incentives to purpose, something echoed by those

who conduct the Dow Sustainability Index, who say that one
best predictors of whether a company takes sustainability seri
whether the CEO and board members have success on that element
as part of their financial remuneration.

When making major decisions, always ask yourself as a leader,
Is this one of those moments of purpose congruence? Would I be proud
to talk about this decision in the same conversation as I discussed our
aspirational purpose? We regularly think of the following words from
John Lockwood, the San Diego city manager in the 1980s (we both
worked for the city, John in the '80s and Jeff in the '90s). Lockwood
had a simple question he would ask leaders about decisions they were
making: "How would you feel explaining this on *60 Minutes* [the most
watched investigative TV show of its day]?" He continued, "If you are
even the slightest bit uncomfortable, you are probably making the
wrong decision in terms of our values."

In a way, each of us as a leader, no matter what our level is, must
ask that simple question: *Is the decision I am making right now in*
congruence with our higher purpose?

PRACTICE 3:
EVERY MESSAGE HAS PURPOSE

One of the key disciplines of purpose-driven leadership is to ensure
that *every* message is connected to purpose. Balance company "margin"
statements with "mission" statements. The typical organization's habit
is to measure, chart, and report solely on operational goals. But many
of us miss the opportunity to do the same with our higher purpose.
We should regularly report on how our business makes a difference
for customers and society. Find the metrics and the stories that bring
the impact on your customer to life. What social and environmental
programs is your company or team part of? Are you trying to reduce
environmental footprint, make a more sustainable supply chain, or
perform work in the community? Convey these stories as often as
you do the ones focused on business success, to provide your team

with a holistic picture of the value your organization delivers both in business and in society.

Message your mission throughout the organization. One large pharmaceutical company does this by posting pictures in its offices of real patients whose lives were saved or made better by the company's medicines. In the halls of buildings across its main campus, one is constantly reminded of the good work the organization does and how it contributes to the well-being of others in a meaningful way. You can't help but feel part of some good greater than yourself.

Use videos to message your mission in action, as well. For one of our health-care clients, we recorded customer stories about the care they received at the hospital, showing examples of the mission in action in all parts of the organization. The videos were then used as part of onboarding to help new employees connect to the organization's higher purpose of providing patient-focused care. The videos were also used to illustrate to employees how their actions make a real difference in the lives of patients and to align all employees to think, feel, and act in ways that promote the deeper mission and purpose of the hospital.

You can do simple things to keep your mission top of mind. For example, at one hospital we worked with in Germany a lullaby plays every time a baby is born. Some Safeway supermarkets make an announcement over the loudspeaker every time an employee collects a donation. The key is to keep the message consistent and to communicate it regularly and clearly, even if it may seem routine or redundant at times.

PRACTICE 4:
EVERY MEETING HAS PURPOSE

The fourth practice for winning in the age of social good is to have mission and purpose as an agenda item in every meeting, no matter the size or the attendees. Use this time to give updates on work, activities, opportunities, and successes related to your purpose. What has your team done recently? In what upcoming opportunities inside or outside the organization can employees participate? What initiatives in the organization are making progress? The leader can take charge of this agenda item, or this duty can be rotated among team members.

Dedicate time in every meeting for someone to tell a story about your purpose in action. At one health-care organization we worked with, employees would regularly share stories of how they were succeeding in their mission, even in small ways. For example, someone mentioned how they'd been impressed by the cooperation across units they'd been observing. Another employee talked about seeing a caregiver spend extra time with a patient who was afraid of an upcoming surgery. A junior nurse told the group that a senior physician, after working unsuccessfully to revive a patient, returned to the unit later to acknowledge the good work of the nurse, praising her efforts in working beside him during a most difficult time.

Use time in meetings to recognize or reward people for their contributions to the company's higher purpose. Just as you acknowledge people for their contributions to projects and operational success, recognize them for their part in serving the mission and purpose. Did someone on your team volunteer on a community project? If so, acknowledge their efforts and talk about how the team is doing great work not only on the job but in the community as well. Give people time in all meetings to share their experiences, what they did, how it made a difference, and how it fits with the organization's mission. Encourage team members to bring in pictures or put together brief presentations about their good work and the impact it has had on them personally.

Build your values into every meeting. Chevron, for example, puts a high value on safety at every level of the organization. One effective way that the company drives this culture is by starting every meeting with a "safety moment"—a brief two- to five-minute presentation reminding workers about safety precautions while on the job and how to avoid potentially harmful incidents. No exceptions—every meeting large or small across the organization has a safety moment.

PRACTICE 5:
HELP EVERY EMPLOYEE SEE IMPACT

Help every team member connect their work to something bigger and see how their contribution makes a difference to the organization's mission and purpose. Use time in your one-on-one meetings with direct reports to discuss how they can connect their personal sense of purpose to their work in the organization. Look for projects, roles, volunteer opportunities, or cross-functional initiatives that would activate your individual employees' sense of purpose and meaning. Make this part of the learning and development discussion as you do with other work skills, competencies, and experiences. Provide opportunities for employees to learn, grow, and contribute to their personal purpose as part of their career path.

Show the positive results of your team's or organization's social or environmental efforts. For example, is your organization active in the community? Set mission goals and milestones, such as 500,000 volunteer hours or 100 local parks cleaned up, then celebrate your achievements with the team or other departments. Help employees feel the positive impact of your mission and values in action. Socialize your mission success and celebrate these milestones. Recognize people and teams who helped out; then make videos and content related to those activities available to employees to share with their network.

PRACTICE 6:
EVERY TEAM HAS A PURPOSE

Develop a compelling and noble team purpose for every team in the organization. Each year dedicate time to building on that purpose and connecting to the company's overall mission. Ask your team honest, hard-hitting questions to get them thinking about purpose: Why do we exist? What value do we add to the organization? To customers? What is our team's contribution to the well-being of society? How do we advance the company's mission and purpose by the work that we do? Push your team to think beyond the numbers to the transcendent qualities of your work.

Discuss your team purpose regularly and set goals and milestones around it as you do with other operational efforts. Have every team member develop a personal purpose statement to connect meaning to the work they perform. On a quarterly or six-month basis, team members should share what gives them meaning and how their work connects them to the mission and purpose of the team and the organization. Be open to employees' personal values and purpose and let them take charge on a cause or mission that they care about. Make it a goal to have one or more of these team members dedicate time to a project that advances the mission and purpose of the organization.

Make it a practice every year to review your company's social, environmental, and community initiatives and connect your team to one or more of these programs. Then scale this idea to the department level: share results across teams at department meetings and with senior leadership. Showcase how your department and teams drive purpose by doing meaningful work and contributing to the organization's mission.

EXERCISE *Every Team Has a Purpose*

Set aside time with your team to have an open discussion about its purpose. This can be done as a stand-alone activity or as part of a team-building retreat.

- Define a team purpose:
  - Why do we exist?
  - How do we make a difference in the community, for society, or for the planet?
  - How do we add value for our customers?
  - How do we contribute to the organization's mission and vision?

- Set purpose goals and measure your purpose.

  - Set goals and milestones around your team's purpose as you do with other operational efforts.

  - Make it a discipline to have contribution goals. For example, commit to 100 hours of community service work each year. Annually, three team members will attend an industry conference or workshop about social or environmental impact and report back to the team.

  - Commit to having one or more team members participate in enterprise-level mission initiatives or programs, such as corporate CSR committees or a task force.

  - Review your scorecard. What can you add or adjust to your metrics or activities to better align with and support the company's CSR strategy and goals?

- Review your company's social and environmental programs annually and look for new ways your team can be involved.

- Give employees time in meetings to share their volunteer efforts.

- Celebrate purpose! Sponsor team celebrations— like a potluck—to recognize purpose milestones or achievements.

PRACTICE 7:
TREAT PURPOSE LIKE IT MATTERS

The seventh practice for winning in the age of social good is to make sure that you treat purpose like it matters. Several years ago we were working with a senior team of a midsized organization who were trying to raise the engagement of their organization in large part by instilling a deeper sense of purpose. At each of our monthly consulting visits, the team was enthusiastic and set ambitious goals.

Five months into the project, the CEO called John and said, "I think we need to end our contract. We have been meeting with you every month for five months, and nothing has changed significantly. People don't seem any more engaged, nor is there any greater passion for purpose among our associates."

Mostly on instinct, John replied, "You know, every time we meet, you and your executive team seem very excited about this effort, but I have noticed that many of the commitments you make don't get followed through on. It makes me wonder: how much do you talk about activating purpose on the other 29 days of a month that we aren't here?"

There was a long silence, followed by a few "um's" and "wells." Finally, the CEO admitted, "We don't meet about this when you aren't here." John then asked how often his team discusses sales, finances, and operational problems. His answer: "Why, almost every day." By that time the CEO had shifted gears. "I get it. If we don't pursue purpose with the same intentional discipline as we do everything else, we can't really expect change."

They didn't fire us but instead lit a fire under their own efforts. They started having a daily 15-minute meeting to ask simply, "What can we do today and this week to drive purpose?" They met every day and hardwired that simple practice into their schedules. Ideas started flowing and engagement went up dramatically—as did company profits.

So, ask yourself: *If I really believe that a revolution is under way right now, am I acting like it?* Think back to our example about the quality revolution. Some companies formed a few task forces, trained people in quality management techniques, and set new goals for quality. But the culture remained hierarchical, quality remained something overseen by the "quality department," and there was often a greater focus on telling customers that our products were great than on doing the hard work to make them great.

The purpose revolution demands commitment, and that requires discipline. Right now there are companies and leaders who will one day be known for having won in the age of social good. The question is whether you will be one of them.

PRACTICE 8:
ACT LIKE YOU CAN CHANGE THE WORLD

Throughout this book we focus on the business imperative of being a purpose-focused organization and leading a culture of purpose. We feel certain that by doing so you will engage the best talent, have an advantage in winning and keeping customers, and increasingly attract investors, who will flock to support you. But the revolution is bigger than all that. The eighth practice is to act like you—and your business—can change the world.

Business has a unique role to play in meeting the challenges facing human society, whether around social justice, environmental sustainability, or a general loss of meaning and community. Often the organizations we work for take up the lion's share of our time and energy, and most major companies do business in numerous countries and often on most continents. If we infuse our teams and our companies with purpose, focusing on creating a better world now and in the future, together we can help solve some of the greatest challenges of our time.

Think, for example, about the impact that you and your business can have on issues like eco-sustainability. When Walmart started pushing its supply chain to be more sustainable, that action reverberated positively around the globe. This one company is having a huge impact on building a sustainable future. Ray Andersen and the team at Interface Carpets not only are close to a zero environmental footprint but have established sustainable practices that are now used widely across the sector. And remember that Ray's personal journey began when a few sales leaders challenged the CEO to form a task group. You can be the person who moves your company to change the world.

When the president decided to pull the United States out of the Paris climate accord in 2017, scores of CEOs and major businesses issued statements saying they intended to continue to lead for a sustainable future and to address climate change. This revolution is not just about getting more business or more engagement; it is about our legacy as leaders.

The revolution is our chance to be part of a new future where purpose permeates work, where business is a force for good, and where each of us becomes happier as well as more connected due to a deep sense that we are doing something important. It won't happen just in large companies but in offices and on shop floors worldwide. You have a part to play in the purpose revolution, and we hope you heed the call and play the part with passion.

TELUS CEO Darren Entwistle put it to us bluntly: "Purpose is not about killing the competitive spirit; it is about getting competitive about doing good. I love being able to tell people that my company has the greenest real estate platform of any company like us." That's what it means to act like you can change the world. Let's all compete to see how much good we can do. In the purpose revolution, that's the competition that matters most.

EXERCISE *How Are You Doing at Leading Purpose?*

As you consider everything you have read and thought about in this book, take a moment now to reflect on your own purpose leadership. For each statement on the following list, give yourself a rating on a scale of 1 to 3—with 1 being *false*, 2 being *somewhat true*, and 3 being *true*.

_____ I regularly talk about my own purpose and values with my team.

_____ I regularly talk about our team purpose and how our work makes a difference.

_____ I make space for purpose in meetings to focus on the impact we have.

_____ I make space for purpose in one-on-one meetings; I dedicate time for team members to talk about the way their work makes a difference.

_____ When motivating people, I work hard to understand how the project or work connects to their values.

_____ I try to fit jobs, roles, and assignments to each team member's values and purpose.

_____ I try to help people find their calling at work; I take time to learn about their values and aspirations and what drives meaning for them.

_____ I help members of my team connect to the higher purpose of their job and tasks.

_____ I connect the work of my team to the company's mission; I talk about the mission and how our team supports it.

_____ I connect the work of my team to the customer; I share stories and information about how our work makes a difference for customers.

_____ I connect the work of my team to the good we do in the community; I talk about how our team contributes to making a difference in society or to the environment.

_____ I recognize people for their work and contributions related to their purpose or values.

_____ I work with my team to set purpose-related goals for the year.

_____ I work with my team to explore the company's social and environmental programs to find new ways for my team to be involved.

_____ I give employees time in meetings to share their volunteer efforts or other purpose-related work.

_____ I celebrate purpose, for example by sponsoring team celebrations or events to acknowledge team efforts to make a difference.

_____ **Total score**

Scoring

16–24: Time to get started on purpose. Look at the list and choose three actions to start with to get focus and traction.

25–35: You are well on your way. To move up, choose three actions to do more of or to start doing.

36–48: Keep up the good work! Look at what you can start doing more of and share what you know.

After you tally your score, consider the following questions:

- What do I do well or do consistently?
- What can I do more of?
- What can I start doing?
- What does my score tell me about how I lead purpose now?
- Where can I focus to get the most traction?

What to Do Right Now

07:49:09

I F YOU HAVE READ TO THIS POINT OF THE BOOK, CONGRATULATIONS! You are now officially far ahead of most leaders, business owners, and entrepreneurs when it comes to being prepared to thrive in the age of social good, and we hope you are eager to get started. We end this book by suggesting *four* things you can do *right now* to begin changing your leadership and your team.

First, if you are like many readers, you read the book on an airplane, on vacation, or around the edges of your life. You got the content but may not have taken the time to do the exercises. Now that you understand the principles and practices, *go back through each chapter and complete the exercises,* taking time to integrate what you have learned. They are all intended to help you apply the content and move toward action.

Second, *find someone with whom to share the ideas* presented throughout the book. There is nothing more challenging and lonely than being one person with new insight into an old system. Research shows that when people are connected to just one other person trying to make similar changes in their life (e.g., losing weight, quitting a bad habit, and so on), they are up to 400 percent more likely to make that change than when going it alone. So, find an ally and do it now. Who else in your organization or circle needs to know what you just learned? Think about who would have the most impact if they knew and, as importantly, who would be receptive to it.

Once you identify that person or group of people, share a summary of what you have learned and focus on the actions you think might make a difference in the context of your organization. Form your own informal purpose accelerator team. Invite each person to read the book and then start meeting to ask, *How can we infuse more purpose in our teams and organization?*

Third, *do something to infuse more purpose in your organization today.* Don't worry about what anyone else is doing or not doing. Don't sit around thinking *If only the CEO, my boss, or my colleagues read this book and took it seriously, something good could happen.* You are an agent of change, and you are the one person you have control over. Start doing something every day to focus more on purpose.

What you do does not need to be major. It could be telling a story about purpose and the difference your work is making, asking a question about what it means to live your company's purpose or values when making decisions, recognizing someone for making a difference (and making a big deal of it), or simply sharing your own purpose with your team and colleagues more boldly. At the end of every day, ask yourself, *What did I do today to grow purpose in my team and my organization?*

Don't worry if your action seems small—just focus on making sure you have done *something* every single day. Each chapter in the book has a list of actions you can take. Choose your five favorites and make your own list to keep on your desk or your smartphone. Look at the list every morning before you start your day and every afternoon before you head out of the office.

Finally, *start tracking your own purpose experience.* Remember, what we pay attention to gets done, so start being attentive to your own moments of purpose. When you realize that you really made a difference for a customer, a client, or a team member or that you contributed to a better society or planet, take a minute to notice how good it feels. Start a journal of some kind, cataloguing your own purpose moments. Being aware of purpose will help it grow, for you and for your team.

And please share your ideas with us! Tell us what's working and what's not. Join the conversation at *purposerevolutionbook.com*. We want to build a movement of leaders who will succeed in business by changing the world. Thanks for joining us.

Notes

INTRODUCTION

Are You Ready for the Purpose Revolution?

1. *The State of the Debate on Purpose in Business*, EY Beacon Institute, 2016, https://webforms.ey.com/Publication/vwLUAssets/ey-the-state-of-the -debate-on-purpose-in-business/$FILE/ey-the-state-of-the-debate-on -purpose-in-business.pdf.

2. Steve Rochlin, Cheryl Yaffe Kiser, Richard Bliss, and Stephen Jordan, *Project ROI Report: Defining the Competitive and Financial Advantages of Corporate Social Responsibility and Sustainability*, IO Sustainability and Lewis Institute for Social Innovation at Babson College, July 9, 2015, https://www.issuelab .org/resource/project-roi-report-defining-the-competitive-and-financial -advantages-of-corporate-responsibility-and-sustainability.html.

3. *The Business Case for Purpose*, Harvard Business Review Publishing, 2015, https://hbr.org/resources/pdfs/comm/ey/19392HBRReportEY.pdf.

4. *Putting Purpose to Work: A Study of Purpose in the Workplace*, PwC.com, 2016, https://www.pwc.com/us/en/purpose-workplace-study.html.

5. *Purpose in Practice: Clarity, Authenticity and the Spectre of Purpose Wash*, Claremont Communications, 2016, http://claremontcomms.com /wp-content/uploads/2016/05/Purpose_In_Practice_Web_Version.pdf.

6. *2016 Workforce Purpose Index: Purpose at Work: The Largest Global Study on the Role of Purpose in the Workforce*, LinkedIn and Imperative, 2016, https:// cdn.imperative.com/media/public/Global_Purpose_Index_2016.pdf.

7. 3BL Media, "Purpose Driven Consumers Planning Sharp Increase in Socially Conscious Purchases: Conscious Consumer Spending Index (#CCSIndex) Establishes Baseline for 2013" (news release), April 3, 2013, http://3blmedia .com/News/Purpose-Driven-Consumers-Planning-Sharp-Increase-Socially -Conscious-Purchases.

8. Nielsen, "Consumer-Goods' Brands That Demonstrate Commitment to Sustainability Outperform Those That Don't" (news release), October 12, 2015, http://www.nielsen.com/us/en/press-room/2015/consumer-goods -brands-that-demonstrate-commitment-to-sustainability-outperform.html.

9. *Five Human Aspirations and the Future of Brands,* GlobeScan, October 6, 2015, https://www.globescan.com/component/edocman/?view=document& id=211&Itemid=591.

10. *Five Human Aspirations.*

11. *Five Human Aspirations.*

12. *Five Human Aspirations.*

13. Unilever, "Report Shows a Third of Consumers Prefer Sustainable Brands" (news release), May 1, 2017, https://www.unilever.com/news/Press -releases/2017/report-shows-a-third-of-consumers-prefer-sustainable -brands.html.

14. Katharina Glac, "The Influence of Shareholders on Corporate Social Respon- sibility" (working paper no. 2, History of Corporate Responsibility Project, Center for Ethical Business Cultures), 2010, http://www.cebcglobal.org /wp-content/uploads/2015/02/Influence_of_Shareholders_on_Corporate _Social_Responsibility.pdf.

15. *The Impact of Sustainable and Responsible Investment,* US SIF Foundation, June 2016, http://www.ussif.org/files/Publications/USSIF_ImpactofSRI _FINAL.pdf.

16. Gregory Unruh, David Kiron, Nina Kruschwitz, Martin Reeves, Holger Rubel, and Alexander Meyer Zum Felde, "Investing for a Sustainable Future," *MIT Sloan Management Review,* May 11, 2016, http://sloanreview.mit.edu /projects/investing-for-a-sustainable-future.

17. Glac, "The Influence of Shareholders."

18. George Serafeim, *The Role of the Corporation in Society: Implications for Investors,* Calvert Research and Management, September 2015, https:// www.calvert.com/includes/loadDocument.php?embed&fn=24319.pdf& dt=fundPDFs.

19. *Report on US Sustainable, Responsible and Impact Investing Trends,* US SIF Foundation, 2016, http://www.ussif.org/trends.

20. "A Survey of Communications: Cutting the Cord," *The Economist,* October 7, 1999, http://www.economist.com/node/246152.

21. "Mobile Subscriptions Q1 2017," Ericsson.com, June 2017, https://www .ericsson.com/assets/local/mobility-report/documents/2017/ericsson -mobility-report-june-2017.pdf.

22. Sun Day Campaign, "Renewable Energy Growth: 40 Years Ahead of EIA's Forecast," EcoWatch.com, May 30, 2017, https://www.ecowatch.com/renew able-energy-growth-eia-2426701265.html.

CHAPTER 1

The Purpose Advantage

1. Steve Rochlin, Cheryl Yaffe Kiser, Richard Bliss, and Stephen Jordan, *Project ROI Report: Defining the Competitive and Financial Advantages of Corporate Social Responsibility and Sustainability,* IO Sustainability and Lewis Institute for Social Innovation at Babson College, July 9, 2015, https://www.issuelab .org/resource/project-roi-report-defining-the-competitive-and-financial -advantages-of-corporate-responsibility-and-sustainability.html.

2. *2016 Workforce Purpose Index: Purpose at Work: The Largest Global Study on the Role of Purpose in the Workforce,* LinkedIn and Imperative, 2016, https:// cdn.imperative.com/media/public/Global_Purpose_Index_2016.pdf.

3. Goodpurpose Study 2012, Edelman, 2012, https://www.edelman.com /insights/intellectual-property/good-purpose.

4. Bill Fischer, "Are Purpose-Driven Leaders the Engine of China's Inno- vation? *Forbes,* June 28, 2015, https://www.forbes.com/sites/billfischer /2015/06/28/are-purpose-driven-leaders-the-engine-of-chinas-new -innovation/#43462da74c1e.

5. Home page, Shinho.com, accessed October 9, 2017, http://shinho.com.cn.

6. "Our Mission," SeventhGeneration.com, accessed September 23, 2017, https://www.seventhgeneration.com/mission.

7. "Laundry Detergent," SeventhGeneration.com, accessed September 23, 2017, https://www.seventhgeneration.com/natural-laundry-detergent?v=31.

8. "Energy Smart Automatic Dishwasher Detergent Gel," SeventhGeneration .com, accessed September 23, 2017, https://www.seventhgeneration.com /energy-smart-automatic-dishwasher-detergent-gel?v=736.

9. "Mission + Action," SeventhGeneration.com, accessed September 23, 2017, https://www.seventhgeneration.com/comeclean.

10. Brian Sozzi, "Starbucks CEO Howard Schultz Stands Up to Trump and Now People Are Calling for Boycotts," TheStreet.com, January 30, 2017, https://www.thestreet.com/story/13970372/1/starbucks-ceo-howard-schultz -stands-up-to-trump-wants-to-hire-10-000-refugees.html.

11. National Institute of Women (INMUJERES) and National Institute of Statistics and Geography (INEGI), *National Survey on the Dynamics of Household Relationships,* 2011, http://en.www.inegi.org.mx/proyectos/enchogares /especiales/endireh/2011.

12. Katy Watson, "Struggling with Sexism in Latin America," BBC.com, August 18, 2015, http://www.bbc.com/news/world-latin-america-33939470.

13. Amy Guthrie, "Heineken Optimistic for More Growth in Mexican Market," *Wall Street Journal,* February 17, 2015, https://www.wsj.com/articles /heineken-optimistic-for-more-growth-in-mexican-market-1424212134.

14. Will Martin, "Brazilian People Drinking Mexican Beer Helped Heineken Have a Bumper Year," *Business Insider,* February 10, 2016, http://www .businessinsider.com/heineken-full-year-results-for-2015-2016-2.

CHAPTER 2

First, Find Your Purpose

1. *2014 Core Beliefs and Culture Survey: Culture of Purpose—Building Business Confidence; Driving Growth,* Deloitte, 2014, https://www2.deloitte .com/content/dam/Deloitte/us/Documents/about-deloitte/us-leadership -2014-core-beliefs-culture-survey-040414.pdf.

2. Jana Kasperkevic, "Wells Fargo Announces Profit Drop after CEO Exits in Fake Accounts Scandal," *The Guardian,* October 14, 2016, https://www

.theguardian.com/business/2016/oct/14/wells-fargo-profits-down-third-quarter-john-stumpf.

3. Wells Fargo, "The Vision and Values of Wells Fargo," March 2017, https://www08.wellsfargomedia.com/assets/pdf/about/corporate/vision-and-values.pdf.

4. Nissan Motor Corporation, "Zero Emission and Zero Fatality," *Nissan Motor Corporation Annual Report 2015,* 2015, http://www.nissan-global.com/EN/DOCUMENT/PDF/AR/2015/AR15_E_P10.pdf.

5. Nissan Motor Corporation, "Our Company: Vision," 2017, http://www.nissan-global.com/EN/COMPANY/MESSAGE/VISION.

6. Tim Maly, "Clever Packaging: Essential Medicine Rides Coke's Distribution into Remote Villages," *Wired,* March 27, 2013, https://www.wired.com/2013/03/colalife-piggybacks-on-coke.

7. Amy Gallo, "The CEO of Coca-Cola on Using the Company's Scale for Good," *Harvard Business Review,* May 29, 2014, https://hbr.org/2014/05/the-ceo-of-coca-cola-on-using-the-companys-scale-for-good.

8. Coca-Cola water stewardship program: http://www.coca-colacompany.com/stories/setting-a-new-goal-for-water-efficiency.

9. Coca-Cola water stewardship program.

10. IBM's Smarter Planet vision is another example of fitting purpose to business: http://www.ibm.com/smarterplanet/us/en.

11. John Mackey and Raj Sisodia, *Conscious Capitalism: Liberating the Heroic Spirit of Business* (Boston: Harvard Business Review Press, 2013).

12. "Our Reason for Being," Patagonia.com, accessed September 24, 2017, http://www.patagonia.com/company-info.html.

CHAPTER 3

Brand Purpose from the Inside Out

1. Sofia Lotto Persio, "Uber Scandal Timeline: Why Did CEO Travis Kalanick Resign?" *Newsweek,* June 21, 2017, http://www.newsweek.com/why-has-uber-ceo-travis-kalanick-resigned-timeline-ride-sharing-apps-pr-woes-627802.

2. Reuters, "Uber Exec Resigns after Sexist Jibe about Women on Boards," *Newsweek,* June 14, 2017, http://www.newsweek.com/uber-head-resigns -board-after-sexist-jibe-about-women-625328.

3. Heather Somerville and Joseph Menn, "Uber CEO Travis Kalanick Resigns under Investor Pressure," Reuters, June 20, 2017, https://www.reuters.com /article/us-uber-ceo-idUSKBN19C0G6.

4. Anita Balakrishnan, "Scandals May Have Knocked $10 Billion off Uber's Value, a Report Says," CNBC.com, April 25, 2017, http://www.cnbc .com/2017/04/25/uber-stock-price-drops-amid-sexism-investigation -greyballing-and-apple-run-in--the-information.html.

5. "56% of Americans Stop Buying from Brands They Believe Are Unethical," Mintel, November 18, 2015, http://www.mintel.com/press-centre/social -and-lifestyle/56-of-americans-stop-buying-from-brands-they-believe -are-unethical.

6. "56% of Americans Stop Buying from Brands They Believe Are Unethical."

7. 2014 Edelman Trust Barometer, Edelman, 2014, https://www.edelman.com /insights/intellectual-property/2014-edelman-trust-barometer.

8. "HP Corporate Objectives and Shared Values," HP.com, accessed September 25, 2017, http://www.hp.com/hpinfo/abouthp/values-objectives.html.

9. "Our Purpose," Manulife.com, accessed September 25, 2017, http://www .manulife.com/Purpose-and-Values.

10. Dan Reed, "United's Response to Sunday's Dragging of a Passenger off a Plane Is Too Little—and Years Too Late," *Forbes,* April 10, 2017, https:// www.forbes.com/sites/danielreed/2017/04/10/uniteds-response-to-sundays -dragging-of-a-passenger-off-a-plane-is-too-little-and-years-too-late /2/#487684a953c6.

11. "Sustainability and Our Future," WholeFoodsMarket.com, 2017, http://www .wholefoodsmarket.com/mission-values/core-values/sustainability-and-our -future#actions.

12. "Sustainability and Our Future," WholeFoodsMarket.com.

13. Tim Moynihan, "Samsung Finally Reveals Why the Note 7 Kept Exploding," *Wired,* January 22, 2017, https://www.wired.com/2017/01/why-the -samsung-galaxy-note-7-kept-exploding.

14. AFP-JIJI, "Samsung Halts Output of Galaxy Note 7, Could Face $2 Billion Recall Cost," *Japan Times,* October 10, 2016, http://www.japantimes.co.jp /news/2016/10/10/business/samsung-halts-output-galaxy-note-7-face-2 -billion-recall-cost.

15. *LRN Ethics Study: Employee Engagement,* LRN, May 30, 2007, http://www .hcca-info.org/Portals/0/PDFs/Resources/library/EmployeeEngagement _LRN.pdf.

16. "Mission Statement," *The Economist,* June 2, 2009, http://www.economist .com/node/13766375.

17. Jixia Yang, Zhi-Xue Zhang, and Anne S. Tsum, "Middle Manager Leadership and Frontline Employee Performance: Bypass, Cascading, and Moderating Effects," *Journal of Management Studies* 47, no. 4 (2010): 654–78. doi: 10.1111/j.1467-6486.2009.00902.x.

CHAPTER 4

Why Most Leaders and Companies Are Failing at Purpose

1. *The Business Case for Purpose,* Harvard Business Review Publishing, 2015, https://hbr.org/resources/pdfs/comm/ey/19392HBRReportEY.pdf.

2. Chris Zook, "How Dell, HP, and Apple Rediscovered Their Founders' Vision," *Harvard Business Review,* July 15, 2016, https://hbr.org/2016/07 /how-dell-hp-and-apple-rediscovered-their-founders-vision.

3. Zook, "How Dell, HP, and Apple Rediscovered Their Founders' Vision."

4. *Five Human Aspirations and the Future of Brands,* GlobeScan, October 6, 2015, https://www.globescan.com/component/edocman/?view=document& id=211&Itemid=591.

5. Leonie Roderick, "Why Brand Purpose Requires More than Just a Snappy Slogan," *Marketing Week,* February 15, 2016, https://www.marketingweek .com/2016/02/15/why-brands-must-prove-their-purpose-beyond-profit.

6. Roderick, "Why Brand Purpose Requires More than Just a Snappy Slogan."

7. Barry Z. Posner and Warren H. Schmidt, "Values Congruence and Differences between the Interplay of Personal and Organizational Value Systems," *Journal of Business Ethics* 12, no. 5 (1993): 341–47. doi: 10.1007/BF00882023.

8. EY Beacon Institute, *How Can Purpose Reveal a Path through Disruption? Mapping the Journey from Rhetoric to Reality,* EY.com, June 2017, https://webforms.ey.com/Publication/vwLUAssets/ey-how-can-purpose-reveal-a-path-through-uncertainty/$File/ey-how-can-purpose-reveal-a-path-through-uncertainty.pdf.

9. Heather Kelly, "Mark Zuckerberg Explains Why He Just Changed Facebook's Mission," CNN.com, June 22, 2017, http://money.cnn.com/2017/06/22/technology/facebook-zuckerberg-interview/index.html.

CHAPTER 5

Every Leader Must Have a Purpose

1. *The Business Case for Purpose,* Harvard Business Review Publishing, 2015, https://hbr.org/resources/pdfs/comm/ey/19392HBRReportEY.pdf.

2. Henri J. M. Nouwen, *The Wounded Healer: Ministry in Contemporary Society* (New York: Image, 1979).

3. Paul Polman, "Business, Society, and the Future of Capitalism," *McKinsey Quarterly,* May 2014, http://www.mckinsey.com/business-functions/sustainability-and-resource-productivity/our-insights/business-society-and-the-future-of-capitalism.

4. Andy Boynton, "Unilever's Paul Polman: CEOs Can't Be 'Slaves' to Shareholders," *Forbes,* July 20, 2015, https://www.forbes.com/sites/andyboynton/2015/07/20/unilevers-paul-polman-ceos-cant-be-slaves-to-shareholders/#5080c14f561e.

5. "More Than Money," *The CEO Magazine,* August–September 2016, http://static.theceomagazine.com/content/downloads/pdf/IND_2016_August_Subhanu_Saxena_CIPLA_Healthcare-Pharmaceutical.pdf.

6. Natalie Fine and Julie Barrier, "When Actions Speak Louder than Words: SAP Recognized as #20 Most Purposeful Brand in the World," SAP, September 30, 2016, http://news.sap.com/when-actions-speak-louder-than-words-sap-recognized-as-20-most-purposeful-brand-in-the-world.

7. Kimberly A. Wade-Benzoni, Leigh Plunkett Tost, Morela Hernandez, and Richard P. Larrick, "It's Only a Matter of Time: Death, Legacies, and

Intergenerational Decisions," *Psychological Science* 23, no. 7 (2012): 704–9. doi: 10.1177/0956797612443967.

8. Otto Scharmer and Katrin Kaufer, *Leading from the Emerging Future: From Ego-System to Eco-System Economies* (San Francisco: Berrett-Koehler, 2013).

CHAPTER 6

Drive Job Purpose, Not Job Function

1. Wiktionary, s.v., "trabajo," last modified July 26, 2017, https://en.wiktionary.org/wiki/trabajo.

2. Kirsten Weir, "More Than Job Satisfaction: Psychologists Are Discovering What Makes Work Meaningful—and How to Create Value in Any Job," *Monitor on Psychology* 44, no. 11 (2013): 39.

3. *The Business Case for Purpose,* Harvard Business Review Publishing, 2015, https://hbr.org/resources/pdfs/comm/ey/19392HBRReportEY.pdf.

4. EY Beacon Institute, *How Can Purpose Reveal a Path through Disruption? Mapping the Journey from Rhetoric to Reality,* EY.com, June 2017, https://webforms.ey.com/Publication/vwLUAssets/ey-how-can-purpose-reveal-a-path-through-uncertainty/$File/ey-how-can-purpose-reveal-a-path-through-uncertainty.pdf.

5. Amy Wrzesniewski, Clark McCauley, Paul Rozin, and Barry Schwartz, "Jobs, Careers, and Callings: People's Relations to Their Work," *Journal of Research in Personality* 31 (1997): 21–33, http://faculty.som.yale.edu/amywrzesniewski/documents/Jobscareersandcallings.pdf. See also Brent D. Rosso, Kathryn H. Dekas, and Amy Wrzesniewski, "On the Meaning of Work: A Theoretical Integration and Review," *Research in Organizational Behavior* 30 (2010): 91–127.

6. Ryan D. Duffy and Bryan J. Dik, "Research on Calling: What Have We Learned and Where Are We Going? *Journal of Vocational Behavior* 83 (2013): 428–36.

7. John Izzo and Eric Klein, *Awakening Corporate Soul: Four Paths to Unleash the Power of People at Work* (Vancouver, BC: FairWinds Press, 1999).

CHAPTER 7

Get Hands-On Purpose

1. "Corporate Culture," Henkle.com, accessed September 20, 2017, http://www
   .henkel.com/company/corporate-culture#Tab-723116_4.

2. Klaus Behrenbeck, "Get the Strategy and the Team Right": An Interview
   with the CEO of Henkel, McKinsey, February 2014, http://www.mckinsey
   .com/industries/consumer-packaged-goods/our-insights/get-the-strategy
   -and-the-team-right-an-interview-with-the-ceo-of-henkel.

3. Jeanne Meister, "The Future of Work: Corporate Social Responsibility
   Attracts Top Talent," Forbes.com, June 7, 2012, https://www.forbes.com
   /sites/jeannemeister/2012/06/07/the-future-of-work-corporate-social
   -responsiblity-attracts-top-talent/2/#3e22105340bc

4. Francine Katsoudas, "A Great Day at Cisco," Cisco Blogs, January 6, 2016,
   https://blogs.cisco.com/news/a-great-day-at-cisco.

5. Cisco, "Cisco Reports Fourth Quarter and Fiscal Year 2015 Earnings" (news
   release), August 12, 2015, https://investor.cisco.com/investor-relations
   /news-and-events/news/news-details/2015/Cisco-Reports-Fourth-Quarter
   -and-Fiscal-Year-2015-Earnings/default.aspx.

6. *LinkedIn Portraits of Purpose Companies: Practical Tips to Hire and Engage
   Talent with Purpose* (LinkedIn Case Study: Kiva), https://business.linkedin
   .com/content/dam/me/business/en-us/talent-solutions/resources/pdfs
   /kiva-purpose-case-study.pdf.

7. Stephanie Vozza, "Why Every Company Should Pay Employees to Volunteer,"
   Fast Company, March 11, 2014. See also *The Purpose-Driven Professional:
   Harnessing the Power of Corporate Social Impact for Talent Development,*
   Deloitte University Press, 2016, https://dupress.deloitte.com/content/dam
   /dup-us-en/articles/harnessing-impact-of-corporate-social-responsibility
   -on-talent/DUP_1286_Purpose-driven-talent_MASTER.pdf.

8. *The Millennial Survey 2014: Big Demands and High Expectations,* Deloitte,
   2014, https://www2.deloitte.com/al/en/pages/about-deloitte/articles/2014
   -millennial-survey-positive-impact.html.

9. "IBM Corporate Service Corps: Overview," IBM.com, accessed September 20,
   2017, https://www.ibm.com/ibm/responsibility/corporateservicecorps.

10. Heineken, "Worlds Apart," published April 25, 2017, https://www.youtube
    .com/watch?v=IbIjGxc1vjo.

11. "History," WarbyParker.com, accessed September 28, 2017, https://www
    .warbyparker.com/history.

CHAPTER 8

Create a Clear Line of Sight to Purpose

1. "Gold Standards," RitzCarlton.com, accessed September 29, 2017, http://
   www.ritzcarlton.com/en/about/gold-standards.

2. "More Than Money," *The CEO Magazine,* August–September 2016, http://
   static.theceomagazine.com/content/downloads/pdf/IND_2016_August
   _Subhanu_Saxena_CIPLA_Healthcare-Pharmaceutical.pdf.

3. "When Life Throws You Lemons: A New York Startup Shakes Up the Insurance Business," *The Economist,* March 9, 2017, https://www.economist
   .com/news/finance-and-economics/21718502-future-insurance-named
   -after-soft-drink-new-york-startup-shakes-up.

4. "How Lemonade Works," Lemonade.com, accessed September 29, 2017,
   https://www.lemonade.com.

5. Frequently Asked Questions: What does the Assessment cover? Impact-
   Assessment.net, accessed October 9, 2017, https://www.bimpactassessment
   .net/how-it-works/frequently-asked-questions/the-b-impact-score#how
   -is-the-assessment-scored.

6. Wikipedia, s.v., "Benefit corporation," last modified August 30, 2017, https://
   en.wikipedia.org/wiki/Benefit_corporation.

7. Wikipedia, "Benefit corporation."

8. "Sustainable Development," Natura website, accessed September 29, 2017,
   https://www.naturabrasil.fr/en/our-values/sustainable-development.

9. "Sustainable Development," Natura website.

10. Gregory Unruh, David Kiron, Nina Kruschwitz, Martin Reeves, Holger
    Rubel, and Alexander Meyer Zum Felde, "Investing for a Sustainable Future,"
    MIT Sloan Management Review, May 11, 2016, http://sloanreview.mit.edu
    /projects/investing-for-a-sustainable-future.

11. *The Impact of Sustainable and Responsible Investment,* US SIF Foundation, June 2016, www.ussif.org/files/Publications/USSIF_ImpactofSRI_FINAL .pdf.

12. *Report on US Sustainable, Responsible and Impact Investing Trends,* US SIF Foundation, 2016, http://www.ussif.org/trends.

13. Gregory Unruh, David Kiron, Nina Kruschwitz, Martin Reeves, Holger Rubel, and Alexander Meyer Zum Felde, "Investing for a Sustainable Future," *MIT Sloan Management Review,* May 11, 2016, http://sloanreview.mit.edu /projects/investing-for-a-sustainable-future.

14. *Tomorrow's Investment Rules 2.0: Emerging Risk and Stranded Assets Have Investors Looking for More from Nonfinancial Reporting,* Ernst & Young, 2015, https://webforms.ey.com/Publication/vwLUAssets/investor_survey/$FILE /CCaSS_Institutional_InvestorSurvey2015.pdf.

CHAPTER 9

How to Win Talent in the Purpose Revolution

1. *Rewriting the Rules for the Digital Age: 2017 Deloitte Global Human Capital Trends,* Deloitte University Press, 2017, https://www2.deloitte.com/content /dam/Deloitte/us/Documents/human-capital/hc-2017-global-human -capital-trends-us.pdf.

2. *The Ultimate Software 2016 National Study on Satisfaction at Work,* Ultimate Software, 2016, https://www.ultimatesoftware.com/happywork. See also *A Global Tolerance Index,* ResearchGate, September 2008, https://www .researchgate.net/publication/241886147_A_Global_Tolerance_Index.

3. *Mind the Gaps: The 2015 Deloitte Millennial Survey,* Deloitte, 2015, https:// www2.deloitte.com/al/en/pages/human-capital/articles/2015-deloitte -millennial-survey.html.

4. *How Millennials Want to Work and Live,* Gallup, 2016, http://www.gallup .com/reports/189830/millennials-work-live.aspx.

5. *Mind the Gaps: The 2015 Deloitte Millennial Survey,* Deloitte, 2015, https:// www2.deloitte.com/al/en/pages/human-capital/articles/2015-deloitte -millennial-survey.html.

6. "A Manifesto," Acumen.org, accessed September 30, 2017, http://acumen.org/manifesto.

7. "Get outta Town: Startup Offers Workers $10,000 If They 'Delocate' from Silicon Valley," *The Guardian,* March 22, 2017, https://www.theguardian.com/us-news/2017/mar/22/zapier-pay-employees-move-silicon-valley-startup.

8. "Create a world that inspires human connection," Airbnb.com, accessed September 30, 2017, https://www.airbnb.com/careers.

9. "Why Work at Dell?" Dell.com, accessed September 30, 2017, http://www.dell.com/learn/us/en/uscorp1/careers.

10. *Rewriting the Rules for the Digital Age: 2017 Deloitte Global Human Capital Trends,* Deloitte University Press, 2017, https://www2.deloitte.com/content/dam/Deloitte/us/Documents/human-capital/hc-2017-global-human-capital-trends-us.pdf.

11. "Glassdoor: Expedia #1 Best Place to Work in the UK 2017," published December 6, 2016, https://www.youtube.com/watch?v=b_H5W4yEncQ.

12. Reid Hoffman, Ben Casnocha, and Chris Yeh, "Tours of Duty: The New Employer-Employee Compact," *Harvard Business Review,* June 2013, https://hbr.org/2013/06/tours-of-duty-the-new-employer-employee-compact.

CHAPTER 10

Eight Practices for Thriving in the Age of Social Good

1. "Organizational Culture Must Be Lived Every Day" (blog), April 1, 2015, Ritz-Carlton Leadership Center website, http://ritzcarltonleadershipcenter.com/2015/04/organizational-culture-is-lived-every-day.

2. "Organizational Culture Must Be Lived Every Day," Ritz-Carlton.

3. Paul Polman, "Business, Society, and the Future of Capitalism," *McKinsey Quarterly,* May 2014, http://www.mckinsey.com/business-functions/sustainability-and-resource-productivity/our-insights/business-society-and-the-future-of-capitalism.

Acknowledgments

John Izzo, PhD

Vancouver, Canada, and Rancho Mirage, California

THIS BOOK HAS BEEN A TWO-YEAR LABOR OF LOVE, RESEARCHING the purpose revolution. Over the past two decades, I have written seven other books, and I can see how many of the people who helped me have been constant over those years. Yet I am grateful that there are always new helpers who show up with each new endeavor.

The first acknowledgment must go to my coauthor, Jeff Vander-wielen. For 25 years we have done good work together, laughed always, and talked about the deepest things. Writing a book with a good friend is always a risk. I am proud to say that we not only wrote something better together but our friendship grew even more through it.

Thanks to Steve Piersanti and the amazing team at Berrett-Koehler. It is so gratifying to be connected to a company that itself is built on the noble purpose to *create a world that works for all.* This is my fifth book with Berrett-Koehler, and their dedication to bringing important ideas to the world continues to inspire me. Thanks to Steve for always helping me improve my ideas and for his ongoing belief in my work.

Thanks to my life partner, Janice Halls, who has always encouraged me to write books and do work that will make the world a better place and people's lives more meaningful. Her infectious smile and sense of humor make my daily life richer, and pushing me to walk the dog with her keeps my eyes up to the joy around me.

Thanks to KoAnn Skrzyniarz and the entire team at Sustainable Brands, who are in the forefront of redefining the good life. Their courage to lead conversations that make a difference helped embolden me to make this book about more than personal happiness. So many great people have come into my life through my association with KoAnn and the purpose-driven companies she brings together in community. Together we are reimagining the good life.

This book would not have been possible without the amazing willingness of so many leaders, companies, and purpose collaborators giving us their time. It would be a big mistake to single out any one company, but throughout these pages you have seen quotes and information from scores of interviews with leaders of amazing companies, including many CEOs and thought leaders.

Among those thought leaders for whom I am most grateful is Andrew Winston, whose passion and courage to speak up about the role business must play to solve our greatest challenges inspires me. Not only is his work making a real difference in moving companies toward creating a sustainable future but the research he and I are doing around CEO commitment (some of which we share in this book) will hopefully nurture more CEO champions. I am deeply appreciative of his work and for opening the doors to some of the most progressive CEOs in the world to share their views with us.

Thanks to Carol Cone and Raphael Bemporad, two purpose pioneers who shared their knowledge with generosity. Thanks also to Bob Willard for his leadership in the sustainability movement and to Jim Kouzes, a friend who has been helping leaders find their best selves for decades.

Thanks to my friends and colleagues at the Learning Network, who always support and challenge me. Although most are writers themselves, they never fail to step up to help in all ways possible. Each one of them will take a call or email anytime to lend advice or simply listen.

Thanks to the great team at Speaker's Spotlight, who continue to promote my work as a speaker. I couldn't ask for better partners, and I look forward to our helping thousands of people find more happiness while building a better world for all.

Thanks to my many friends new and old, who fill my life with so much joy. You know who you are, and I would not want to leave anyone out. Special thanks always to my brother from another mother, Jeremy Ball. We have worked long hours together to help awaken the soul, and I hope we will do so for many more. An extra nod to David Kuhl and Matthew Quetton, who both inspire me with their own gifts and enrich me with their friendship. Julie Sedger is a soul sister and has shown that she is there whenever needed. To Cindy Camberg and Ken Lasser—old friends are often the very best—thanks for lasting the test of time.

Throughout my life I have had the fortune to know numerous mentors who embodied a purpose-focused life. Among them I give thanks for the late Reverend Dr. Robert Kelley, who first saw in me the potential to inspire and who inspired me with his servant leadership, and to John Mroz, who took his purpose to help bridge differences and wound up influencing history at the EastWest Institute. John, the world could sure use you now.

Finally, and by far the most thanks, to my mother, Irene Parisi-Izzo, who left this world for the next this past spring. I know how proud you are that I used my gifts and talents in the pursuit of good. Though I miss you incredibly every single day, I know you are, as you told me near your dying breath, watching over me still. Your final week of courageous grace will never be forgotten.

Jeff Vanderwielen, PhD

San Diego, California, and Pickerel Lake, Townsend, Wisconsin

I WISH TO ACKNOWLEDGE MY GOOD FRIEND, COLLEAGUE, AND coauthor John Izzo. For more than 25 years, I have had the privilege to work with John to make a difference in business and society. He has always been a great inspiration, and this work has deepened our friendship and connection to one another.

The book would not have found its way to press without the support and genius of Steve Piersanti and Jeevan Sivasubramaniam at Berrett-Koehler. Their unwavering commitment to the book and its importance to business and society kept us energized, focused, and moving forward.

I am grateful to David Moldawer, who helped shape the original manuscript, and to Zach Gajewski, for his invaluable efforts to shape and refine the content and flow of the book. Not only was Zach a pleasure to work with, but his editorial contributions pushed the book to another level.

Thank you to my wife, Yulia, for her insight and encouragement. Her bright ideas seeded during breakfast chats and long talks into the evening dot the book like beautiful flowers coloring the textual landscape.

All of the good and meaningful work we do happens within a community of family and friends—we never walk the path alone. I want thank my close family for their love and for always believing in me. Thanks also to my friends Michael, Jeff, Scott, Blair, and Jeannie, who continually stimulate my intellectual curiosity and are always there for me throughout the ups and downs of life. I've been blessed with a community that consistently reminds me to reach beyond myself to embrace a higher purpose and contribute to a larger good.

Index

About the Authors

John Izzo is a best-selling author, executive coach, thought leader, and sought-after speaker on leadership, employee engagement, corporate culture, sustainability, and purpose. Each year he speaks to more than 75 corporate and association gatherings around the globe, exhorting leaders to step up to the challenges of our time. He is known for his hard-hitting keynote speeches that offer inspiring and practical advice on how to lead in the emerging world of work.

Dr. Izzo is the author of eight books, including *Awakening Corporate Soul, Values Shift, Stepping Up,* and *The Five Secrets You Must Discover Before You Die.* He was a pioneer in the corporate social responsibility movement and a prominent voice on shifting expectations among employees and customers.

Over the past 25 years, he has spoken to more than a million people, taught at three major universities, coached hundreds of executives, and helped more than 600 organizations effect sustainable culture change. His clients have included Walmart, TELUS, Clorox, Coca-Cola, Manulife, RBC, Qantas, Fairmont, Lockheed Martin, Boeing, IBM, Microsoft, SAP, Ford, DSW, Air Canada, Humana, and the Mayo Clinic. His work has been featured by CNN, *Fast Company,* CBC, the *Wall Street Journal, Inc.,* and the *New York Times.*

Dr. Izzo holds a BA in sociology from Hofstra University, master's degrees in theology and psychology, and a PhD from Kent State University. He has served on the boards of numerous large nonprofits and is currently on the advisory board for Sustainable Brands, the world's leading community of purpose-driven companies. He is an adjunct professor at the University of British Columbia.

Dr. Izzo splits his time between Vancouver, Canada, and Southern California.

Contacting Dr. Izzo

To contact Dr. Izzo or to book a speaking engagement, write to john@drjohnizzo.com.

Visit His Website

www.drjohnizzo.com

Follow Him on Twitter

@DrJohnIzzo

LinkedIn

www.linkedin.com/in/drjohnizzo

Jeff Vanderwielen is vice president of consulting at Izzo Associates and an organization development expert who translates emerging trends in the sustainability and purpose landscape into actionable, results-driven initiatives for clients. He brings 20-plus years of experience helping global organizations articulate a compelling purpose— their core good—as the organizing center for their vision, strategy, and culture.

Dr. Vanderwielen has facilitated hundreds of interactive workshops with top organizations, using simulations, stories, and iterative engagement processes to help leaders learn by doing. He is a former consultant with Ernst & Young and brings extensive experience as a coach to global leaders, facilitating strategic planning and helping organizations manage complex change efforts. His clients have included

Chevron, Conagra Brands, Merck, Northrop Grumman, UBS, Amgen, Kellogg, BC Hydro, Exxon, Ascension Health, Sustainable Brands, Gateway, Trinity Health, SDG&E, and UC San Diego Medical Center.

Dr. Vanderwielen holds an MS in clinical psychology from the University of Idaho and a PhD in organizational psychology from the California School of Professional Psychology.

He lives in San Diego, California, with his wife, Yulia, and is the father of two adult daughters.

Contacting Dr. Vanderwielen
jvzgroup@gmail.com
LinkedIn
www.linkedin.com/in/jeff-vanderwielen-phd-5342a11

Also by John Izzo, PhD
The Five Thieves of Happiness

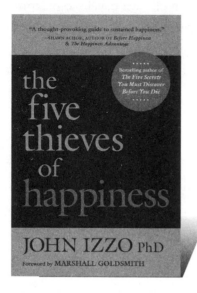

Happiness is our natural state, for each of us and for humanity as a whole, argues John Izzo. But that happiness is being stolen by insidious mental patterns that he depicts as thieves: the thief of control, the thief of conceit, the thief of coveting, the thief of consumption, and the thief of comfort. He discovered these thieves as he sought the true source of happiness during a year-long sabbatical, walking the Camino de Santiago in Spain and living in the Andes of Peru. This thoughtful and inspiring book describes the disguises these thieves wear, the tools they use to break into our hearts, and how to lock them out once and for all. This book will help us all discover, develop, and defend the happiness that is our true nature while creating a world we all want to live in.

Paperback, 160 pages, ISBN 978-1-62656-932-4
PDF ebook, ISBN 978-1-62656-933-1
ePub ISBN 978-1-62656-934-8
Digital audio ISBN 978-1-62656-931-7

Berrett–Koehler Publishers, Inc.
www.bkconnection.com   **800.929.2929**

The Five Secrets You Must Discover Before You Die

Based on a highly acclaimed public television series, this inspiring book reveals the keys to lasting happiness gleaned from the author's interviews with more than 200 people, ages 60 to 106, who were identified by friends and acquaintances as "the one person they knew who had found happiness and meaning." From town barbers to Holocaust survivors, from aboriginal chiefs to CEOs, they answered questions like, What brought you the greatest joy? What do you wish you had learned sooner? What ultimately mattered and what didn't? Here Izzo shares their stories—funny, moving, and thought-provoking—and the Five Secrets they revealed. This book will make you laugh, move you to tears, and inspire you to discover what matters long before you die.

Paperback, 200 pages, ISBN 978-1-57675-475-7
PDF ebook, ISBN 978-1-57675-551-8
ePub ISBN 978-1-60509-531-8

Berrett–Koehler Publishers, Inc.
www.bkconnection.com

800.929.2929

Stepping Up
How Taking Responsibility Changes Everything

Stepping Up argues that almost every problem, from personal difficulties and business challenges to social issues, can be solved if all of us look to ourselves to create change rather than looking to others. By seeing ourselves as agents of change we feel happier, less stressed, and more powerful. John Izzo offers seven compelling principles that enable anyone, anywhere, anytime to effectively bring about positive change. And the book is filled with stories that will inspire you: a middle-aged Italian shopkeeper who fought back against the Mafia, two teenagers who took a stand and ignited an antibullying movement, an executive who turned a dying division into a profit center, and many more. We all have the power to change the world—John Izzo shows us how.

Paperback, 184 pages, ISBN 978-1-60994-057-7
PDF ebook, ISBN 978-1-60994-058-4
ePub ISBN 978-1-60994-059-1

Berrett–Koehler Publishers, Inc.
www.bkconnection.com

800.929.2929

Berrett–Koehler
Publishers

Berrett-Koehler is an independent publisher dedicated to an ambitious mission: Connecting people and ideas to create a world that works for all.

We believe that the solutions to the world's problems will come from all of us, working at all levels: in our organizations, in our society, and in our own lives. Our BK Business books help people make their organizations more humane, democratic, diverse, and effective (we don't think there's any contradiction there). Our BK Currents books offer pathways to creating a more just, equitable, and sustainable society. Our BK Life books help people create positive change in their lives and align their personal practices with their aspirations for a better world.

All of our books are designed to bring people seeking positive change together around the ideas that empower them to see and shape the world in a new way.

And we strive to practice what we preach. At the core of our approach is Stewardship, a deep sense of responsibility to administer the company for the benefit of all of our stakeholder groups including authors, customers, employees, investors, service providers, and the communities and environment around us. Everything we do is built around this and our other key values of quality, partnership, inclusion, and sustainability.

This is why we are both a B-Corporation and a California Benefit Corporation—a certification and a for-profit legal status that require us to adhere to the highest standards for corporate, social, and environmental performance.

We are grateful to our readers, authors, and other friends of the company who consider themselves to be part of the BK Community. We hope that you, too, will join us in our mission.

A BK Business Book

We hope you enjoy this BK Business book. BK Business books pioneer new leadership and management practices and socially responsible approaches to business. They are designed to provide you with groundbreaking and practical tools to transform your work and organizations while upholding the triple bottom line of people, planet, and profits. High-five!

To find out more, visit **www.bkconnection.com**.

Berrett–Koehler
Publishers

Connecting people and ideas
to create a world that works for all

Dear Reader,

Thank you for picking up this book and joining our worldwide community of Berrett-Koehler readers. We share ideas that bring positive change into people's lives, organizations, and society.

To welcome you, we'd like to offer you a free e-book. You can pick from among twelve of our bestselling books by entering the promotional code **BKP92E** here: http://www.bkconnection.com/welcome.

When you claim your free e-book, we'll also send you a copy of our e-news-letter, the *BK Communiqué*. Although you're free to unsubscribe, there are many benefits to sticking around. In every issue of our newsletter you'll find

- A free e-book
- Tips from famous authors
- Discounts on spotlight titles
- Hilarious insider publishing news
- A chance to win a prize for answering a riddle

Best of all, our readers tell us, "Your newsletter is the only one I actually read." So claim your gift today, and please stay in touch!

Sincerely,

Charlotte Ashlock
Steward of the BK Website

Questions? Comments? Contact me at bkcommunity@bkpub.com.

MIX
Paper from
responsible sources
FSC® C002589

Certified

Corporation
bcorporation.net